Generis
PUBLISHING

Justice in the Crossfire: Courts, Conflict, and the Anglophone Crisis in Cameroon

One Judge's Lived Experience

Judge Mukete Tahle Itoe

Title: Justice in the Crossfire: Courts, Conflict, and the Anglophone Crisis in Cameroon

One Judge's Lived Experience

ISBN: 979-8-89966-395-6

Author: Judge Mukete Tahle Itoe

Cover image: https://unsplash.com/

Publisher: Generis Publishing
Online orders: www.generis-publishing.com
Contact email: info@generis-publishing.com

Table of Contents

Dedication

This book is dedicated to the brave men and women of Cameroon's judiciary, lawyers, and ordinary citizens who, despite adversity, continue to uphold the principles of justice. It is also for all those whose voices remain unheard in the pursuit of fairness, equity, and the rule of law.

Acknowledgments

I wish to express my profound gratitude to all those who have contributed, directly or indirectly, to this work. I am especially indebted to the judicial officers, lawyers, and civil society actors who shared their experiences and insights, providing invaluable perspectives on the challenges facing Cameroon's justice system.

My thanks also go to colleagues, mentors, and friends whose encouragement and constructive critiques strengthened the clarity and depth of this book.

Finally, I acknowledge my family particularly my wife, Eveline, and children, Bosambe, Damian, and Pascal, for their constant support throughout this project. Their encouragement has been a source of inspiration and sustenance. Any merit in this work belongs to all who strive for the preservation of justice but any shortcoming is mine alone.

Preface

In the serene backdrop of Cameroon's picturesque landscapes, a profound tragedy unfolds—a tapestry woven with threads of hope, despair, justice, and conflict. Nowhere is this more apparent than in the Anglophone regions, where once-thriving communities grapple with the ripple effects of a crisis that has transformed their reality. As I embark on the journey of unraveling the complexities of justice in the crossfire of this ongoing turmoil, I invite you to walk alongside me through stories laden with grief, resilience, and an indomitable pursuit for justice. This book aims not only to illuminate the legal struggles faced by countless individuals but also to probe the very essence of what it means to live in a society where the principles of law and order have been so grievously upended.

The narrative you are about to engage with is not merely an account of a legal system under siege but serves as a mirror reflecting the fabric of a society facing the harsh consequences of division and conflict. The Anglophone crisis is more than a political dispute- it is a humanitarian catastrophe that has reverberated through the lives of ordinary citizens, lawyers, judges, and activists—all striving to carve out a semblance of justice amid the chaos. Historical grievances have ignited a combustion of hostility, leading to clashes that have fundamentally altered the landscape of not only the Anglophone regions but the country at large. With each passing day, the rule of law, often considered the bedrock of civilized society, finds itself increasingly eroded, leaving the most vulnerable susceptible to myriad injustices.

Through the pages that follow, you will encounter the heart-wrenching stories of individuals like the displaced judicial officer who once commanded respect within the walls of a venerable court, now rendered powerless, struggling to reclaim the dignity of their profession against a backdrop of fear and uncertainty. You will meet the litigants, whose voices have been stifled, witnessing firsthand the innumerable barriers that now obstruct their paths to justice. As I weave these narratives together, I hope to imbue each tale with a sense of urgency—a reminder that access to justice is not a privilege, but a fundamental human right that must be asserted and defended, even in the most trying circumstances.

Moreover, this exploration delves into the lives of determined lawyers and tireless workers of civil society organizations (CSOs) who confront the climate of fear and intimidation with bravery and tenacity. Their stories are emblematic of a deeper truth—that the quest for justice is often paved with personal sacrifices and tribulations, demonstrating humanity's capacity for empathy and solidarity in the face of adversity. These advocates possess a unique understanding of the societal implications at stake and the critical need for a functioning judiciary that can uphold the principles of fairness, due process, and accountability. Their unwavering commitment to restoring the rule of law stands as a beacon of hope for those whose lives have been upended by the chaos surrounding them.

The challenges described in this book are not merely localized, but resonate on a global scale, presenting stark reminders of the fragility of justice systems in conflict zones around the world. Each chapter will invite you to reflect on the significance of justice as the linchpin of social order. The insights gleaned from the Anglophone crisis implore us to recognize that the breakdown of legal institutions reverberates far beyond the courtroom—touching upon the fundamental principles of human rights and community resilience. Conflict may wreak havoc on infrastructure and lives, yet, the human spirit's capacity to adapt, fight back, and advocate for change can reignite the flicker of hope in the darkest of times.

In conclusion, this book aspires not only to document the systemic failures that have emerged but also to catalyze a vital conversation surrounding the necessary reforms required to strengthen the judiciary in Cameroon. As we delve into the implications of the weakened legal framework and explore potential pathways toward restoration and healing, I urge you to consider your role in this narrative. Every account shared within these pages is a call to action, an appeal for solidarity with those caught in the crossfire of conflict, and a reminder of the collective responsibility we share to ensure that justice is not merely an ideal, but a lived reality for all.

With every page you turn, may you feel the pulse of resilience, the ache of injustice, and the call to advocate for a future where the rule of law reigns supreme, reigniting the hope for a more just and equitable society. Welcome to "Justice in the Crossfire"—a narrative that aspires to transform, engage, and ultimately empower us all in the noble pursuit of justice.

Mukete Tahle Itoe, PhD
Bamenda, Cameroon

Foreword

In *Justice in the Crossfire: Courts, Conflict, and the Anglophone Crisis in Cameroon*, Judge Mukete Tahle Itoe delivers a deeply insightful and courageous examination of one of the most distressing realities confronting Cameroon's legal landscape—the erosion of judicial order and access to justice in times of conflict, focusing on the ongoing secessionist conflict in the English-speaking Northwest and Southwest regions. Drawing on his extensive judicial experience and his formidable scholarship in international law, Judge Mukete presents a rare and authoritative perspective on how the ideals of justice are tested when courts fall silent and the rule of law is strained to its limits, as has occurred during this conflict between armed separatist groups and state security forces from 2017 to date.

What distinguishes this work is its delicate balance between critical reflection and constructive vision. Without descending into politics or blame, the author exposes the silent suffering of a justice system caught between turbulence and resilience. He documents how courtrooms have become inaccessible, Magistrates displaced, and litigants deprived of their constitutional right to be heard during the current crisis—revealing the human and institutional toll of prolonged instability on the administration of justice.

Judge Mukete's writing is both analytical and humane. He speaks as a witness and participant in the struggle to preserve the integrity of the law in the midst of the insecurity and institutional paralysis currently being experienced in the English-speaking regions. Through meticulous analysis and thoughtful observation, he reminds us that when the justice system falters, peace and accountability grow distant. Yet, through reform, resilience, and moral courage, restoration remains possible.

This book stands as both a mirror and a guide—a mirror reflecting the painful realities faced by Cameroon's courts in the English-speaking regions, and a guide illuminating the path toward renewal. *Justice in the Crossfire* is a timely and indispensable contribution to legal scholarship and judicial reform. It reinforces Judge Mukete Tahle Itoe's reputation as one of Cameroon's foremost jurist-scholars, whose intellectual rigor and moral clarity continue to shape the pursuit of justice in the country and beyond.

I commend this important work to all who believe that justice—though often tested—is the surest foundation of peace and civilization.

Gordon Crawford
Professor of Global Development
Centre for Peace and Security
Coventry University, UK

Chapter 1:

Introduction to the Anglophone Crisis

1.1 Historical Context

In the heart of Central Africa lies Cameroon, a nation rich in cultural diversity and historical complexity. Its colonial legacy has forged a fascinating yet troubling trajectory that continues to shape its socio-political landscape. To understand the lamentations and conflicts of today's Anglophone population, one must delve deeply into the historical roots that planted the seeds of discontent. Cameroon's journey began in the late 19th century when European powers, driven by imperial ambitions, carved up the continent without regard for the existing ethnology-linguistic divisions. France and Britain emerged as the primary colonial powers in Cameroon, a territory that became a football in the geopolitical machinations of colonial competition. The division of the land into French and English sectors in 1916, following World War I, sowed the first discord among the inhabitants. The British controlled the Northwest and Southwest regions, known today for their Anglophone identity, while the French dominated the rest of the country. This division was not merely geographical but seeped into the very core of the identity of the people, introducing a dichotomy that would amplify grievances for decades to come.

With the advent of independence in the early 1960s, the two colonial territories were united to form the Republic of Cameroon, but the process was anything but seamless. The British Southern Cameroons gained independence and subsequently joined *La République du Cameroun* in a unification that was marred by promises unfulfilled. The union, heralded as a step toward cooperation and mutual benefit, soon revealed deep-seated disparities as the Anglophone regions found themselves increasingly marginalized in both political and socioeconomic spheres. The Francophone-dominated government centralized authority in

Yaoundé, leaving Anglophone voices muffled and sidelined. In this atmosphere, the perception of Anglophones as second-class citizens took root, fueling resentment and frustration towards a government that seemed indifferent, if not hostile, to their rights and needs. Educational policies, language rights, and the judicial system became focal points of contention. The imposition of the French legal system on the Anglophone judiciary, which had previously operated under English common law, was particularly jarring. Legal practitioners and citizens alike were thrust into a confusing quagmire where their rights to a fair trial and legal representation were compromised, amplifying the feelings of injustice that festered within the community.

As the years progressed, the Anglophone frustrations coalesced into organized demands for increased autonomy and rights. This culminated in demonstrations and peaceful protests in the late 2016 and early 2017 period, where citizens took to the streets to express their grievances, demanding a return to the Anglo-Saxon legal and educational systems. However, the response from the government was heavy-handed, dismissive of the legitimate calls for reform and dialogue. The harsh crackdowns on these peaceful protests catalyzed a spiraling cycle of conflict, as the populace felt further alienated, pushing some toward radicalization. The emergence of separatist groups, who called for the creation of an independent state known as *Ambazonia*, marked a watershed moment in Cameroonian history. This divergence from peaceful advocacy to armed conflict transformed the scenario, intertwining the desperate quest for rights with the brutal realities of civil unrest and violence. The government's counteractions included militarization of the Anglophone regions, leading to increased casualties and displacement among civilians. The intermingling of military aggressiveness with everyday life left an indelible mark on the community, where fears and traumas began to overshadow aspirations for justice and normalcy.

In this chaos, the judiciary found itself in an increasingly precarious position. Courts that were once centers to resolve disputes and uphold citizen rights became targets in the eyes of the combatants. Court buildings were attacked, judges and lawyers became victims of intimidation, and many clients were obstinately denied the right to legal representation. The legal system, which ought to have been a bastion of justice for the citizens, turned into another casualty of the conflict, contributing to a pervasive climate of lawlessness. This legal vacuum forced civilians, often unfairly accused or victimized, to navigate an atmosphere rife with fear, distrust, and uncertainty. Tales of individuals either seeking recourse or victims trying to seek justice for wrongs endured warrant acknowledgment, as their stories encapsulate the grave implications of a disrupted legal framework.

Within this intricate historical narrative, the role of civil society also deserves mention. Non-governmental organizations championed the causes of the marginalized, working tirelessly to revive the discourse around peace and justice. They became lifelines for many, striving to document abuses and advocate for victims' rights. Their efforts often faced challenges, whether from the government's resistance to change or the complexities of operating in a space fraught with danger. Nonetheless, these players in the civil society space emphasized the importance of human rights at the local, national, and international levels. However, as violence escalated, their challenges compounded, leading to increased vulnerability and risks related to advocacy work in an unstable environment.

The historical context of the Anglophone crisis in Cameroon reveals a complex web of delays, disregard, and ultimately disruption that culminated in a full-blown conflict with dire implications for justice. As grievances transformed into sustained conflict and the judiciary crumbled under the pressure, individuals faced untold hardships, enduring a system that had become a paradox in which justice was simultaneously sought and denied. In literature and activism, these struggles are interwoven into the regional narrative, transcending mere history and emerging as calls to action for grounding the vital discussion around state reform, community resilience, and a profound understanding of what justice truly signifies. Thus, the Anglophone crisis is not just a chapter in Cameroon's tumultuous history but reflects the universal quest for dignity, rights, and equity in the face of an unforgiving societal landscape, enshrining the need for ongoing dialogue and reform that preserves the integrity of the judiciary and reaffirms the pillars of justice for all.

1.2 Political Tensions

The political tensions in Cameroon, particularly between the Anglophone regions and the central government, are deeply rooted in a historical context characterized by marginalization, neglect, and a series of failures to address the genuine concerns of the English-speaking population. Since the reunification of Cameroon in 1961, the political landscape has been fraught with disparities and grievances that have significantly influenced the dynamics between the Anglophone communities and the Francophone central authority. For decades, Anglophone Cameroonians have voiced their displeasure over their perceived second-class status within a predominantly Francophone state. This enduring sense of disenfranchisement dramatically accelerated in recent years, as various socio-political and economic grievances surged to the forefront, igniting a conflict that runs deep into the fabric of Cameroonian society and directly impacting the judicial system.

At the heart of the political tensions lies the contrasting linguistic and cultural identities of the Anglophone regions, composed mainly of the Northwest and Southwest regions, and the Francophone areas. The imposition of a centralized governmental structure that emphasizes the French language and culture has fostered an environment in which Anglophone Cameroonians feel alienated and sidelined. This marginalization has perpetuated a cycle of resentment that has only intensified over the years. Several key events have punctuated this historical trajectory, including the contentious debates over the education system, legal reforms, and the governance model. For instance, in 2016, the Anglophone lawyers and teachers' unions protested against the use of French in courts and schools, presenting a concentrated expression of their refusal to conform to a legal and educational system that ignored their linguistic heritage and culture. Rather than addressing these legitimate grievances, the government responded with a heavy-handed crackdown, exacerbating the already simmering tensions and leading to protests that spiraled into violent confrontations.

As the situation continued to deteriorate, the Anglophone crisis took on a multifaceted character, encompassing issues of governance, human rights, and the very essence of citizenship. The grievances evolved beyond mere linguistic concerns, transforming into a broader demand for autonomy and recognition of Anglophone rights within the state. This escalated conflict culminated in the declaration of independence by separatist groups, further deepening the chasm between the Anglophone population and the central government. The subsequent militarization of the conflict has had catastrophic implications for access to justice, with state forces accused of excessive violence against civilians, arbitrary detention, and violations of basic human rights. The judiciary, once a bastion for the protection of rights and ethics, found itself ensnared in this web of conflict, its personnel targeted, its structures destroyed, and its very purpose usurped by a security-eccentric approach adopted by the government.

Within this context of strife, the judiciary's role has morphed from that of an impartial arbiter to a pawn in the political theater dominated by the executive. The deterioration of judicial independence has produced an environment where fear permeates the very essence of legal practice. Judicial officers share harrowing accounts of intimidation and threats that have forced many to abandon their posts, while those remaining struggle to maintain any semblance of order in a system that has been rendered dysfunctional. Courts are no longer venues where justice is served, but rather places where despair reigns, exacerbated by the systematic dismantling of legal protections that underpin a functional justice system. This erosion has profound consequences not just for those pursuing justice, but also for the entire socio-political ecosystem in the Anglophone regions. Litigants face insurmountable barriers, often caught in a vicious cycle of injustice, as their fundamental rights are disregarded, and legal recourse remains beyond their reach.

Moreover, the role of local and international actors plays a crucial part in shaping the political tensions surrounding the Anglophone crisis. Civil society groups, community leaders, and the diaspora have continually amplified the voices of Anglophone Cameroonians, seeking accountability from the government while striving to shed light on the ongoing human rights abuses. However, these efforts face not only governmental resistance but also the heaviness of international indifference. The international community's response has been limited, often mired in political complexities that fail to recognize the urgent need for intervention. Many advocacy groups highlight the plight of the Anglophone regions in reports and discussions, yet tangible actions remain lacking. The narrative presented by these actors often collides with the government's portrayal of the conflict, painting the situation as a mere law-and-order issue rather than a deep-seated political crisis. This dichotomy complicates the quest for solutions and underscores the essential need for dialogue that is not only a façade but a genuine effort to address the core issues confronting the Anglophone population.

As the political landscape continues to evolve, one cannot overlook the resilience of the Anglophone people in the midst of these tensions. Community leaders, legal practitioners, and ordinary citizens demonstrate an admirable dedication to preserving their identity and rights, often at personal risk. Stories of protest, activism, and grassroots movements highlight a vibrant civil society pushing back against oppression, motivated by a shared vision for a just and equitable future. These community responses underscore a vital truth: the pursuit of justice is not merely about legalities but it is an intrinsic aspect of human dignity. While the political atmosphere remains volatile, the indomitable spirit of the Anglophone population serves as a beacon of hope for the restoration of justice and recognition in the years to come.

In conclusion, the political tensions between the Anglophone regions and the central government reflect a complex tapestry woven with historical injustices, identity conflicts, and systemic failures in governance. The unfolding crisis, centered on the rights and dignity of citizens, has reached a critical juncture that demands urgent attention. As we navigate the path forward, it becomes increasingly imperative to address these political dynamics to restore the rule of law and ensure the protection of human rights for all Cameroonians, particularly those in the Anglophone regions. Understanding these intricacies provides an essential foundation for advocates, legal practitioners, and policymakers to engage effectively with stakeholders in a collective endeavor to forge a more just and equitable society. Ultimately, the resolution of this conflict and the restoration of judicial integrity hinge upon an unwavering commitment to dialogue, accountability, and the upholding of the principles that define a functioning democracy.

1.3 Impact on Society

The Anglophone crisis in Cameroon has wrought profound changes to the daily lives of citizens, reshaping the very fabric of communities that once flourished with a sense of shared identity and purpose. The grievances of the Anglophone population, which began as a chorus of discontent over perceived marginalization, have escalated into a conflict that has transformed once-peaceful neighborhoods into battlegrounds, where fear and uncertainty now reign supreme. This shift has been insidious, creeping into the lives of ordinary people and displacing not only the institutions they relied upon but also the very essence of their collective existence. With every clash between government forces and separatists, echoes of a broken promise fill the air, and the daily rhythm of life is interrupted by the cacophony of gunfire and the haunting wails of those who mourn.

The economic fabric of these regions has frayed, leading to a situation where livelihoods have been severely compromised. The vibrant marketplace that once bustled with the sounds of bargaining and laughter has become eerily quiet, as traders flee from the violence or are unable to cross checkpoints imposed by either state or non-state actors. Farmers no longer tend to their fields, paralyzed by fear of attacks or the inability to transport their goods to market. It is not merely the loss of income that shakes the foundation of these communities but it is the erosion of trust, the belief that neighbors can still care for one another even in the presence of chaos. Families are torn apart, as children are left to fend for themselves, often becoming entangled in the conflicts as they seek to protect their homes or avenge their losses. For many young people, the conflict has robbed them of their innocence; schools shuttered or turned into makeshift barracks render any semblance of normalcy a distant memory. Education, a tool that was once envisioned as a ladder to upward mobility, now stands as a bleak reminder of lost opportunities, creating a generation bereft of the knowledge and skills necessary to thrive.

Psychological trauma runs rampant among those who survive, with the scars of violence etched deeply into the psyche of parents whose children have been lost to senseless acts of brutality. Countless testimonies of survivors reveal a shared sense of hopelessness, as families struggle to rebuild amid the rubble of their dreams. The anguish of being unable to secure justice for wrongful acts exacerbates the emotional strain. They find themselves in a system that offers little recourse and a society that has become polarized. Some citizens, once hopeful advocates for progress, now sit in the shadows, fearful that any expression of dissent might lead to violence or imprisonment. The very act of seeking justice becomes a dangerous endeavour, as those who dare to confront the eroding rule of law face intimidation, threats, and even violence. Legal practitioners, once bastions of support for community members seeking redress, are equally ensnared in this web of fear. Many have fled or altered their practice to avoid drawing fire from both the authorities and armed groups.

Communities that once thrived on solidarity now find themselves divided, with neighbors turning against neighbors based on political affiliations or differing opinions on the path forward. Stories abound of families torn apart, of once-close friends rendered strangers by ideology, and loyalties forged in communal struggles placed under unbearable strain. The fabric of trust that wove these societies together frays in the stark light of conflict. Institutions meant to uphold justice, such as courts and legal frameworks, have become resounding echoes of what was once a functioning system, dismantled by ongoing violence and pervasive corruption. When people seek legal recourse for injustices, they are often met with a bureaucratic labyrinth where dangers lurk at every corner. The hopelessness is palpable, a resignation to a cycle of abuse that reinvents itself day after day.

Yet, within the confines of despair, there emerges a glimmer of community resilience. Individuals and organizations rise to the occasion, spearheading efforts to restore that sense of moral order, even amid the chaos. Grassroots movements defy the odds, working diligently to provide support to those affected by the crisis, whether that be through legal aid, psychological counseling, or simply a listening ear. Local activists emerge, often at great personal risk, seeking to bridge divides and unite a fractured populace. Their courage inspires those around them to recommit to the principle that justice is not simply a luxury reserved for the privileged but a fundamental right that must be acknowledged and pursued by all. These heroes often work in the shadows, battling for recognition of human rights and dignity while contending with a backdrop of violence that seeks to silence them.

Access to basic services, such as healthcare and education, has become a challenge as people in conflict zones find themselves in dire need, often without hope of receiving assistance or care. Health facilities are not immune. Many have been damaged or are operating at reduced capacity, leaving vulnerable populations to reckon with diseases that would have previously been preventable. In such dire circumstances, the resilience of these communities shines through in indomitable spirit, as citizens band together to offer mutual support, sharing limited resources to care for the wounded and the sick, creating makeshift classrooms in homes, and instilling hope despite the harrowing circumstances.

In conclusion, the impact of the Anglophone crisis on the daily lives of citizens is profound and far-reaching, reshaping communities in ways that are not only tangible but deeply emotional. Young lives are disrupted, social fabrics are torn, economic stability is destabilized, and the very ideals of justice and rule of law are cast aside in a maelstrom of conflict. Yet, in the thick of the trials, moments of resilience flicker, as communities rally together in defiance of the chaos, seeking to reclaim their agency and restore justice to a world that seems to have forgotten its value.

Chapter 2:

Disruption in the Administration of Justice

2.1 Closure of Courts

In the heart of the Anglophone regions of Cameroon, the physical closure of courts stands as a stark testament to the broader upheaval that has characterized daily life amid the ongoing conflict. The closures are not merely an administrative inconvenience but they represent a profound disruption in the fabric of justice, dismantling the fundamental principles that govern society. Once bustling with activity, courthouses that served as bastions of legal resolution have become derelict buildings, a haunting reminder of the societal collapse that accompanies violence and instability. The closure of these judicial institutions is multifaceted, rooted in the direct threats faced by judicial officers, the escalating violence spurred by the conflict, and the palpable fear that now surrounds the very concept of law and order.

Judges and court staff, once dedicated to the impartial administration of justice, have found themselves displaced from their roles and, for many, their homes. The sense of normalcy that characterized their professional lives has been swept away, replaced by uncertainty and trauma. Many have fled to safer regions, their professional lives abruptly interrupted, as they become witnesses to the very collapse of the judicial structures they once served. Those who remained in the embattled regions often reported threats to their safety, with armed groups asserting dominance and rendering it physically dangerous to fulfill their duties. This forced exodus has not only stripped the courts of their personnel but has also eroded the public's trust in the legal system, creating a void where the rule of law should prevail. For ordinary citizens, the closure of courts signifies an end to hope—a sentiment often encapsulated in their testimonials, where they express the desperation of seeking justice in a system that no longer functions. The barriers to justice have grown insurmountable. Court dates are postponed indefinitely, essential legal filings are left unaddressed, and the legal recourse that citizens once took for granted has transformed into an elusive dream. With court buildings shuttered and judges seeking refuge, a just resolution to disputes becomes an impossibility, leading many to resort to informal or extrajudicial methods to settle conflicts, further complicating the already fragile societal situation.

Moreover, the implications of court closures extend beyond the immediate loss of legal services but they seep into the very psyche of communities that have historically relied on the judiciary as a stabilizing force. The absence of courts fosters an environment of lawlessness, where vigilante justice can take root, and the lines between right and wrong blur. Community members are left to navigate their grievances without the mediating presence of the law, often yielding to the highest bidder or the most intimidating voice, circumventing the rule of law in favor of the whims of men wielding power. The situation is dire but as clashes continue between separatists and government forces, the once-pristine image of justice has been tarnished, leading to a growing acceptance that violence may be the only recourse left available to those wronged. This corresponds with increased reports of human rights abuses—arbitrary detentions, torture, and extrajudicial killings. Civilians are caught in the crossfire, suffering agonies that are compounded by the realization that no legal remedy exists for them, further entrenching their disenfranchisement from a system that was designed to protect and empower them.

The closure of courts also aggravates the plight of legal practitioners who strive to maintain their integrity in a system under siege. Lawyers, once regarded as champions of justice, now face dire conditions that test their resilience and dedication to their profession. Many have found their offices deserted, their livelihoods hanging by a thread as cases languish without resolution, potential clients frightened away by the pervasive violence. Those who risk the journey to provide legal counsel do so at significant personal cost, often facing harassment from armed groups or the state itself. The emotional toll of witnessing the deterioration of their profession weighs heavily on these practitioners—what was once a noble calling rooted in the pursuit of justice has been transformed into an environment filled with anxiety and risk. All too frequently, lawyers share stories of having to abandon their clients due to the instability of the courts, a grim reflection of the reality where helplessness has become the norm.

Caught in this storm, ordinary citizens are left grappling with the fallout. Victims of crimes, whether brutal assaults or petty disputes, show resilience tempered by despair as they navigate the complexities of seeking justice in a system that has all but ceased to function. Testimonials emerge revealing heart-wrenching tales of desperation, often tinged with a sense of betrayal—their rights to due process, to fair trials, to legal representation now only distant memories. One particularly poignant case involved a young woman who had endured a violent assault in the town of Batibo. With the courts closed, she recounted her harrowing experience trying to navigate a legal labyrinth that had disintegrated. Each visit to what was once the courthouse reminded her not just of her trauma but of the absence of recourse. She spoke of the threats she faced from her assailant, emboldened by the knowledge that there would be no legal repercussions, no authorities willing to intervene.

As time stretches on with the courts shuttered, the implications of these closures multiply, laying waste to the very notion of justice and contributing to the normalization of impunity. The community's ability to resolve disputes peacefully erodes further, casting a long shadow over aspirations for stability and peace. The rhetoric surrounding justice becomes muddled, as all parties in the conflict increasingly view law not as a route for resolution, but as a hindrance to their objectives, further entrenching divisions and hostility. The societal rift deepens, leaving individuals to wander through a landscape devoid of the legal safeguards that once provided a semblance of order and protection. The callous neglect of the judiciary echoes throughout the Anglophone regions, where the closure of courts signifies more than just the suspension of legal activities— it embodies the loss of hope and the chilling silence that now permeates the pursuit of justice. As communities search for meaning and resolution in the midst of disorder, the echoes of closure reverberate, urging those in power to recognize the critical need for rebuilding, reforming, and restoring faith in a system that has been irrevocably altered. Without such efforts, the pathway to justice remains obscured, buried beneath the weight of closed doors and the silence of an absent judiciary, leaving behind a legacy of despair—not just for today, but for generations to come.

2.2 Judicial Displacement

The Anglophone crisis in Cameroon has led to a significant and distressing phenomenon: the displacement of judges and legal staff, an outcome that reverberates through the very fabric of the judicial system. The trajectory of this displacement is not merely a byproduct of conflict but rather, it is emblematic of a systematic breakdown of the rule of law. In regions that once boasted operational courts, the echoes of gavel strikes and the rustling of legal documents have been replaced by an unnerving silence, a palpable testament to the void left in the wake of unrest. As government forces and separatists collide, the justice systems that are meant to uphold order and fairness are dismantled, leaving judges and court personnel vulnerable to threats, violence, and trepidation. This displacement not only signals the physical removal of legal practitioners from their posts but it illustrates a much deeper and more troubling reality where the principles of justice become incidental to the prevailing chaos.

Judges, the custodians of the law, find themselves in precarious situations, often forced to abandon their posts to escape imminent danger. Reports abound of judicial officers who have fled their jurisdictions, leaving behind their chambers and responsibilities. They are not simply uprooted from their positions but are compelled to navigate treacherous paths through conflict-ridden landscapes, seeking refuge in areas deemed safer. The psychological toll of such displacement is profound, as these individuals grapple with the loss of their professional identities and the disheartening realization that their vocations, which once resonated with a sense of purpose and dignity, now feel stained by fear and insecurity. As they seek solace in unfamiliar surroundings, the very foundations of their roles crumble, resulting in a justice system that is left adrift and hindered from functioning.

Many judges have detailed their harrowing experiences in seeking safety, recounting how their homes were ransacked, their courtrooms transformed into battlegrounds, and their lives threatened by both state and non-state actors. The streets that once welcomed them into the corridors of justice have now morphed into avenues of fear, where the law holds no sanctity. The displacement of these legal professionals is often accompanied by the closure of courthouses, and courtrooms that previously served as sanctuaries for the oppressed have fallen silent. Structures that housed adjudications, diatribes, and defenses, where rights were asserted and liberties defended, now stand as ghostly monuments to a past where justice was delivered with sincerity and commitment. The closing of these courthouses reflects a systemic prioritization of security over justice, where the mere threat of violence renders the sanctity of the judicial process obsolete.

The impact of this judicial displacement is felt far beyond the individual circumstances of judges and legal staff. It has cascaded into a crisis of access to justice for ordinary citizens who find themselves bereft of the legal representation they so desperately require. Litigants, who once considered the courthouse a refuge for their grievances, are left stranded in a marginal state, unable to navigate their disputes in a system that has effectively collapsed. The lack of accessible legal recourse aggravates the already dire situation faced by communities grappling with the effects of the conflict. Women seeking redress from domestic abuse, families yearning for justice after the loss of loved ones, and individuals wrongfully accused are all thrust into a void where lawful processes have been benched by the specter of violence.

While the physical displacement of judges and court personnel captures attention, it is imperative to note the broader implications on legal ethics and the integrity of the judicial profession. The perception of the judiciary as an unbiased and competent arbiter of justice is at risk, as the absence of judges and the suspension of legal services exacerbate public distrust in a system they already view as flawed. When the entities entrusted with protecting citizens' rights are absent due to conflict, it creates a chasm that can be exploited by those wishing to evade accountability. Thus, positions of power and authority may become supplanted by vigilante forms of justice or arbitrary violence, wherein individuals take matters into their own hands, further eroding the social contract that underpins civilized existence.

Those displaced from the judiciary often find themselves in the trenches of civil society, working with NGOs and advocacy groups to continue their fight for justice, albeit from a position significantly weakened by their displacement. They share poignant narratives of resilience, reaffirming their commitments to the rule of law even in the face of overwhelming odds. These displaced judicial officers become beacons of hope, utilizing whatever platforms available to process grievances and combat injustices perpetuated in their absence. Yet, the bittersweet irony lies in their forced adaptation to roles that were traditionally beyond their remit, as they transform from judges to activists, an evolution dictated by circumstances rather than career choice. The resourcefulness often exhibited by these individuals speaks volumes to their dedication to the principles of justice, even as the structures they once upheld stand in ruin.

Rebuilding a functional judiciary in the Anglophone regions will undoubtedly require substantial time and effort. Addressing the issue of displaced judges and court personnel is pivotal to restoring the faith of citizens in the legal system. Initiatives aimed at reintegrating these professionals back into the justice sector will be necessary. However, such endeavors must be rooted in a sincere commitment to security, ethical governance, and impartiality. Only when judges return to their posts, free from the shackles of fear and insecurity, can the courts begin to reclaim their roles in delivering timely justice. A multi-faceted approach that encompasses training, psychological support, and community engagement will be integral to this task. The path towards reconstituting a resilient judiciary hinge on acknowledging the sacrifices made by those who have endured displacement and crafting environments conducive to their return.

As the chapters of this narrative unfold, it is crucial to recognize that the challenges presented by judicial displacement during the Anglophone crisis serve as both a cautionary tale and a rallying cry for reform. The indomitable spirit of those who persevere despite overwhelming adversity reveals the potential for renewal and change within a system that currently teeters on the brink of collapse. As discussions regarding the future of the judiciary emerge, stakeholders must remain vigilant in ensuring that the sacrifices of the displaced are not in vain and that the urgency of crafting effective responses to this crisis does not diminish. Building bridges toward justice will demand conscientious efforts, empathy, and a collective realization that at the heart of every displaced judge and legal staff member lies a story—a story deserving of recognition, justice, and ultimately, a restored sense of purpose within a fractured system.

2.3 Inaccessibility for Litigants

In the landscape of conflict, access to justice often hangs precariously in the balance, teetering on the edge of despair as citizens grapple with the cruel realities that have unfolded in Cameroon's Anglophone regions. The ongoing strife has cast a long shadow over the legal system, creating an environment where seeking redress through the courts has morphed into an arduous, and oftentimes impossible, task for many who once believed in the sanctity and reliability of judicial recourse. As the echoes of gunfire and the anxiety of unrest reverberate through the streets, the places where justice was once dispensed—the courthouses—now stand largely abandoned and silent, their doors barred not just by locks but by the chilling fear that grips both citizens and judicial officers alike.

The displacement of judges and court staff, coupled with the destruction of vital court infrastructure, have combined to raise formidable barriers for those who continue to cling to the hope of a fair trial and an equitable resolution to their grievances.

For many litigants, the physical inaccessibility of courts can be traced back to the very fabric of their disrupted lives. As violence escalated between government forces and separatists, judicial officers found themselves in a precarious position. For instance, a once-respected judge, now displaced, recounts how the conflict disrupted his life—one day, he was presiding over cases in a bustling courtroom, and the next, he was fleeing for safety, leaving behind the legal proceedings of countless individuals who depended on him. Such displacement has not been a singular event but it has swept through communities like wildfire, scattering legal professionals across the country and beyond, often leading to abandoned positions in courts that once served as beacons of hope. The inability of judges to fulfill their roles has created a nightmare scenario for litigants, many of whom find themselves facing an endless loop of uncertainty. With courts shuttered, or operating minimally under duress, ordinary citizens are left to navigate a system that feels foreign and unwelcoming in their time of need.

As the very institutions meant to protect and uphold the law falter, the implications for the average person seeking justice become increasingly dire. Families who once lived their lives with some semblance of stability now feel the relentless weight of injustice as their cases—often deeply personal matters potentially involving land disputes, domestic violence, and other human rights violations—are left unresolved during the mayhem. In one particularly heartbreaking case, a woman arrives at what was once her local courthouse in the town of Tombel, only to find it closed, its windows shattered and its walls marked by the passing of time and torment. Instead of receiving guidance or support, she is met with the stark reality that her voice will not be heard, her pain disregarded as the systems she once relied upon have crumbled around her. The court closures are more than simple logistical challenges but they represent a fundamental realignment of the power dynamics within society, as desperation and despair set in for those who find themselves deprived of the very means to seek justice.

In addition to the physical barriers, the psychological toll of the conflict has imposed a heavy burden on potential litigants. Fear pervades the atmosphere, creating a chilling effect on those who might otherwise have sought the judicial system for resolution. The omnipresent threat of violence hangs like a dark cloud, leading individuals to doubt the safety of courtrooms that should symbolize refuge and fairness. Many are unwilling to approach courthouses, fearing that their participation in legal proceedings could expose them to further retaliation or intimidation from armed groups, both state and non-state actors. The stories of individuals who have confronted these fears and dared to seek justice come with harrowing accounts of harassment, threats, and violence—stories that resonate as cautionary tales throughout the population. With each anecdote, the message becomes clear: accessing the courts is not merely a matter of navigating procedural barriers but it hinges on the very ability to survive in the midst of an environment rife with danger.

Furthermore, the disconnect between the legal framework and the realities faced by litigants becomes acutely evident in the distressing experiences of those attempting to secure legal representation. Many lawyers, faced with the imperatives of their personal safety and the realities of their precarious professional circumstances, have similarly fled, leaving behind a critical void in legal advocacy and assistance that exacerbates the difficulties faced by citizens. As citizens attempt to find a grounded footing within a collapsing system, they find that the few practicing lawyers who remain often do so under extreme duress, working in fear of both physical harm and the repercussions of representing vulnerable clients. This reduction in legal representation creates a ripple effect, further isolating individuals from avenues of redress and exacerbating the sense of hopelessness that pervades the Anglophone regions.

Considering these interlaced layers of injustice and barriers, it becomes increasingly evident that the path to creating a functional judicial environment in these conflict-affected areas will not be straightforward. Elaborate reform strategies must be established, prioritizing the empowerment of legal practitioners and the restoration of lost infrastructure. To effectively reinstate the judiciary as a pillar of societal stability, the legal processes must be accompanied by efforts to ensure the safety of those who seek to offer support and assistance. Initiatives geared towards establishing mobile courts, community mediation programs, or even reaching out to displaced judicial officers through digital means could serve as effective stopgaps while prioritizing longer-term solutions.

In summary, the inaccessibility for litigants in Cameroon's Anglophone regions is a multifaceted crisis, deeply intertwined with the broader themes of conflict and its consequences on the fabric of society. The erasure of trust in the judicial system, coupled with fear and structural impediments, creates a reality where the quest for justice feels not merely hindered, but utterly inaccessible. As this book unfolds, it highlights not only the urgent need for reform but also the resilience and determination of the communities caught in the crossfire—a testament to their unyielding desire for justice, an essential element of their humanity, despite the harrowing constraints imposed by their environment.

Chapter 3:

Voices of Legal Practitioners

3.1 Threats and Intimidation

In the midst of the Anglophone crisis in Cameroon, the atmosphere is thick with fear, palpable in every legal office and courtroom where justice is expected to reign but instead finds itself beleaguered by threats and intimidation. Legal practitioners, who once presumed their roles as guardians of the law and defenders of rights, now navigate a treacherous landscape riddled with peril. As I sit across from Solange, a resilient lawyer in Ndop,who has devoted her life to championing the underprivileged, the weight of her stories hangs heavily in the air. Her voice trembles slightly as she recounts her experience of being threatened. "It began subtly," she reflects, "the phone calls in the middle of the night, the whispers in the shadows outside my house. At first, I brushed them aside, thinking it was just paranoia. But as I took on more cases related to the separatists and the injustices they faced, it became all too real." Solange describes the escalation of intimidation tactics employed by those who do not wish for her client's voices to be heard in the judicial system. She articulates the chilling reality of how legal professionals like herself have become the targets of both state and non-state actors, fearing that their attempts to advocate for justice may attract violent retribution.

Mokube, another legal advisor based in the town of Muyuka, offers a harrowing narrative of a close encounter with the dark side of this conflict. Following the legal representation of detained activists, he became an unwilling protagonist in a terrifying saga. "I received an anonymous letter," he explains, his eyes darkening as he recalls the moment. "It said I would face dire consequences if I continued to represent those involved in the separatist movement." The fear that envelopes Mokube is not just his own but it is a fear that permeates his firm and the legal community as a whole. Gangs of armed vigilantes have stormed into courthouses, demanding to know who is assisting detainees, turning what should be sanctuaries of justice into battlegrounds. The intimidation tactics stretch into the very fabric of their daily existence, discouraging attorneys from taking on cases that need their expertise the most. The message from these suitors of violence is straightforward: defend the downtrodden and face retaliation, simply for exercising what should be a fundamental right—representing one's client with integrity and courage.

In such adversity, the stories of Parfait, an experienced judicial officer, resonate profoundly. Describing his own journey through threats aimed at silencing him, he reveals the mental strain they induce. "I had to hide my identity more times than I can count," he confides. "I cover my face while taking public transport, fearful of being recognized." Parfait is clear about the consequences of this intimidation: it has created a chilling effect, where many lawyers are compelled to retreat to safer, quieter practices, abandoning cases that align with their commitment to human rights due to the very real prospect of danger. The children they once dreamt of helping remain unrepresented and unheard amid the cacophony of the crisis. Their advocacy is stymied by the ever-present threat of violence and harassment, raising the stakes for those who dare to stand against the tide of oppression.

As these practitioners navigate their precarious reality, the protective measures they have instituted begin to feel like a cage rather than a safety net. For example, Aissatou, an attorney known for her fierce dedication to social justice, shares how she constantly re-evaluates her surroundings. "I have started working from home mostly. I realized I could not afford to stay in the office late anymore, even though it meant taking a hit to my productivity," she shares, voice low and pensive. The confluence of these experiences presents a grim picture of a legal landscape where the continuous threat of violence looms large over the pursuit of justice. This environment leads to a slow erosion of the principles of due process that should be the bedrock of any legal system. The presence of fear manifests in a reluctance among young, ambitious lawyers to enter the profession altogether.

They witness the toll on their more seasoned counterparts and hesitate to engage with a system marred by violence and intimidation.

In the face of such adversity, solidarity among legal practitioners has become critical. Many uphold informal networks for support; lawyers helping one another with advice on furthering personal safety or means of representation while evading threats. But even this camaraderie comes with its own risks, as any association with individuals marked as dangerous figures can invoke suspicion and danger from both sides of a divided society. Frustration turns to desperation in these legal chambers, where discussions of strategy must intertwine with survival tactics. I can see the weight of the world in the expressions of those assembled, teachers of the law wrestling not only with the intricacies of their cases but with the threat of retribution for standing up for what is right. This perilous dance between action and caution complicates their fight for justice, overshadowing even the most basic legal processes with dread.

In the light of their experiences, it becomes clear that the heart of the crisis lies not only in the legal battles being fought but, in the individuals, —the lawyers, judges, and citizens—thrust on the front-line. As these practitioners strive to navigate the fragmented legal terrain, they share an unspoken bond forged through shared tribulation. Their narratives echo the fundamental tenet of human rights—an individual's right to fair representation. However, the prevailing violent rhetoric forces them to ask with increasing despair: Is that right worth fighting for? And at what cost? The chilling impact of these threats infuses every corner of their pursuit of justice, weighing not just on the individual, but collectively diminishing the foundations of the legal system itself.

It becomes glaringly evident that intimidation operates as a powerful tool to dismantle all that they work to protect. As such, the need for a robust response to these threats is urgent. The lack of governmental backing for the safety of legal practitioners only reinforces a climate in which fear reigns supreme. The absence of investigations into threats and attacks on lawyers further exacerbates the challenges they face. Those who are meant to uphold the law find themselves at the mercy of a fractured system, where their pursuit of justice can quickly spiral into a journey of self-preservation. Their stories are cries for help, underscoring the dire need for both the local and international community to respond. Every narrative punctuates a long-standing plea for the restoration of order and safety within the judicial system—a plea that hinges on the belief that justice is not merely an ideal to be aspired to, but a collective obligation to be fulfilled, no matter the cost.

Within each tale of intimidation lies a compendium of resilience, threaded through the unwavering determination of legal practitioners refusing to be silenced. They strive to make an indelible mark on history, one case at a time, evoking both admiration and heartbreak. In doing so, they exemplify the duality of anguish and hope that accompanies the quest for justice in the conflict zones. Their courage illuminates the path forward, inspiring a movement not only for justice but for the security of all those involved in the legal process. Indeed, in the shadow of threats and intimidation, the legal fraternity in Cameroon stands as a testament to perseverance, tirelessly advocating for the justice that eludes so many, and fervently striving for a restoration of the rule of law that is desperately needed. In revealing the painful realities of their struggles, these practitioners are not merely recounting experiences but they are also crystallizing a vision for a more just society, a society where the rule of law is a shield instead of a source of vulnerability.

3.2 Resistance and Resilience

In the heart of conflict-torn regions, where darkness looms over the legal landscape, a relentless spirit of resistance and resilience shines through the indomitable courage of lawyers who refuse to abandon justice, even in the face of grave dangers. The stories of these legal practitioners paint a vivid picture of a profession steeped in complexity, where the pursuit of justice is often met with hostility and violent repercussions. They do not merely represent a profession but they embody a profound commitment to the principles of law, order, and humanity. The journey of these brave lawyers, whose narratives emerge from the ruins of a fractured judicial system, serves as a testament to their unwavering dedication to their clients and the values that shape civil society.

Across the Anglophone regions of Cameroon, as violence erupted and the clashing of arms echoed through the streets, countless legal practitioners found themselves entrenched in a battle that extended far beyond traditional courtroom duels. With each client they represent, they take on not just a case, but the oppressive weight of systemic injustices exacerbated by the conflict. Among them is Saman, a seasoned lawyer who has spent years navigating the treacherous waters of a flawed justice system. "Every time I step outside my house, I am reminded of the risks," Saman shares, a mixture of resolve and weariness painted on his face. He recounts the many instances where he has received threats, sometimes veiled and other times explicit, urging him to abandon cases involving political dissent or allegations against state agents. Yet, the fear he faces only fuels his commitment to justice. "The clients I represent often have no one else; they are vulnerable, and it is my duty to stand for them." Saman's resolve is shared by many of his colleagues, whose testimonies reveal a communal bond of camaraderie forged through shared experiences of intimidation but also strengthened by unwavering conviction toward securing access to justice.

Another compelling narrative arises from Julia, a young lawyer whose fervent spirit took root in the pursuit of human rights advocacy. Julia places her hands firmly on her desk, eyes alight with a mixture of passion and concern as she recounts her experiences of navigating a legal minefield. Representing individuals who have endured extrajudicial detentions or torture at the hands of security forces, she knows that merely speaking truth to power involves considerable risk. "I have been in situations where I was followed, my communications monitored, and my life threatened," she affirms, pride in her work evident even when recounting tales of fear. But she also emphasizes how community support has become a vital lifeline. Lawyers, rights activists, and civilians alike rallying together to support each other's causes, creating a clandestine network of solidarity in the chaotic landscape. Julia often reflects upon the courage demonstrated by clients who stand before her, vulnerable yet tenacious, and claims that her motivation is drawn from their strength. "Each time I prepare for a hearing, I think of their stories, their suffering. It becomes a source of strength for me. It reminds me of why I began this journey." Thus, Julia emerges as both a defender of rights and a beacon of hope, representing the possibility of resilience that can outlast oppression.

The risk to these lawyers is not merely theoretical but it is visceral, as threats often materialize in forms that shake the very foundation of their resolve. The accounts of intimidation at the hands of security forces paint a grim yet illuminating picture.

The harrowing story of Abel, an attorney with a reputation for his ferocity in championing human rights, stands out sharply. As he recalls an incident where he and his colleagues were ambushed while attempting to deliver legal aid to detainees in the town of Fundong, there is an undeniable tremor in his voice. "They surrounded us, shouting, they wanted to intimidate and scare us," he recalls. But even as fear gripped him in that moment, he explains how they persevered, refusing to be driven away from their civic duty. "We were there for the people who had no voice. Our clients depended on us, and in that moment, we became their voice." Such acts of defiance are not merely acts of individual courage; they symbolize a collective opposition against an oppressive regime. The acts of resistance by these legal practitioners are woven together, becoming part of a broader narrative that seeks to challenge the status quo and demand accountability.

These practitioners, exemplifying the spirit of resistance, draw upon various sources of support that bolster their endeavors. Legal civil society organizations (CSOs) such as the Refugee Welfare Association Cameroon

(REWAC)[1], play a crucial role in fortifying their work, providing not only logistical assistance but also ensuring that their rights and safety are safeguarded. Collaborating with civil society organizations has helped create platforms through which lawyers can document abuses and advocate for reforms without fear of immediate repercussions.

The experiences of Marlene, an NGO worker dedicated to advancing legal rights for marginalized populations, intersect poignantly with those of the lawyers she assists. "We empower them, help them to communicate, and ensure that they have access to safe spaces to discuss strategies," she notes, emphasizing the urgency of collective efforts to secure a healthier justice ecosystem during times of crisis. The synergy between these legal practitioners and support organizations fosters environments where even amid unrest, the quest for justice can continue, intertwining strands of resistance with communal support.

Lawyers in the Anglophone regions have not only demonstrated resilience through their actions but they embody the notion of advocacy as a holistic approach, where understanding the socio-economic conditions that plague their clients becomes imperative to their legal strategies. Awareness of the hardships that marginalized communities face has animated their advocacy, subtly shifting from traditional litigation to also encompassing educational outreach and public awareness campaigns within their communities.

For instance, Sarah, a community lawyer, has organized workshops aimed not only at legal literacy but also at empowering citizens to exercise their rights. "Most people do not even know their rights, let alone how to seek justice. By equipping them with knowledge, we are fostering resilience at the community level," she emphasizes. The embedding of legal knowledge within communities reflects a forward-looking vision, where resilience is not solely a lawyer's burden but a collective responsibility that she hopes will lead to systemic change.

[1] Website: www.rewac.org.

Even as systemic transitions remain skeptically slow, the resolve of these legal practitioners reminds us of the intricacies of human motivation and the relentless ambition to strive for justice even in dire straits. Interviews with victims of injustice, who share their personal stories of struggle and triumph in the face of adversity, reveal the profound impact that dedicated lawyers can have on their lives. Sarah's work is evident as she recounts the day that she successfully advocated for the release of a man wrongfully accused of collaboration with armed groups. The man's profound gratitude and tears stirred a deep sense of fulfillment within her. "It is moments like these that empower us to continue," Sarah shares, reflecting on how each victory, however small, creates ripples of resistance against systemic breakdown.

Despite the threats and violence that loom overhead, these lawyers stand as unwavering pillars of hope, illustrating that around the wreckage of a collapsed system, the seeds of resilience can still take root and flourish. Their narratives paint a dynamic tapestry of resistance encapsulated in the fabric of their dedication, a celebration of human tenacity against overwhelming odds. The determination to fight for justice, serving their clients and the community at large, persist even as the specter of intimidation challenges their journey. Therein lies the essence of their stories: of unwavering commitment that transcends individual ambitions, reflecting a profound desire for justice that encompasses not only their roles as lawyers but also their shared humanity. In the chaotic aftermath of conflict, the heroism of these legal practitioners stands out, inspiring hope for a future where justice prevails and the rule of law is restored, serving as a reminder to society that the quest for justice knows no bounds, even during crossfire.

3.3 Case Studies

In the Anglophone crisis in Cameroon, legal practitioners have found themselves operating in a perilous environment where their commitment to justice is both noble and fraught with danger. The narratives of these brave individuals reveal the gravity of the situation, showcasing both their resilience and the harrowing realities they encounter. One such lawyer, Emmanuel, recounts his experience in representing a group of peaceful protesters who had gathered to express their dissent against government policies that marginalized the English-speaking regions. In the eyes of the state, these individuals were classified as enemies, leading to their arbitrary arrests and brutal detentions. Emmanuel recalls how, despite the risks, he felt compelled to defend their rights, viewing his role not simply as an attorney, but as a guardian of their dignity. As he ventured to the detention center to seek access to his clients, he was met with hostility from military personnel who viewed his efforts with suspicion. His voice trembled with intensity as he described the threats he received, each one serving as a grim reminder of the stakes involved in his work. Still, he persisted, harnessing the power of the law as a tool to challenge unlawful detentions, understanding that every success, no matter how small, could serve as a beacon of hope.

Another harrowing tale comes from Patricia, a female lawyer who has specialized in human rights cases within the context of the ongoing crisis. Patricia's path to justice often diverges sharply from the ideals she had once envisioned in her legal education. Once, she had taken pride in representing individuals against police abuse. However, the Anglophone crisis has dramatically colored that narrative. While she remained dedicated to her clientele, she faced the constant threat of being targeted not just for her advocacy but for her very gender in a patriarchal society riddled with violence. Meeting with victims became a clandestine operation, often taking place in safe houses or abandoned buildings to avoid detection by the authorities. She describes one case wherein a young woman named Amina had been subjected to violence during a police raid on her home. Patricia, moved by Amina's anguish, took it upon herself to bring the case to court, despite the high probability of retaliation from the police. But as she navigated through what felt like a legal labyrinth, the barriers only multiplied: intimidation from police officers during court hearings, judges who refused to confront state abuses, and a pervasive atmosphere of fear that loomed over the courtroom like a dark cloud. It was during one of these hearings that Patricia experienced firsthand the haunting silence that fell over the room as intimidating figures from the government loomed near, their presence a stark reminder of the much larger power dynamics at play. Each time she stood to speak, she grappled with the knowledge that her voice could be silenced, that justice might never be served, yet she felt a duty to advocate for those silenced before her.

In another corner of the crisis, we meet George, a judicial officer who witnessed the destruction of the very institutions he served. His story encapsulates the chaos that ensued when the armed conflict escalated, effectively rendering the courts inaccessible for many. The courthouse where George had operated underwent a bloody transformation. Windows shattered and walls defaced became a symbol not only of the ongoing violence but of the rampant impunity that flourished in its wake. He recalls moments filled with exhilaration when he had presided over cases that could change lives, dispelling justice like a beacon of hope during troubled times. However, the moment separatists took a stand against governmental authority, he became a target. A relentless campaign of violence and intimidation was unleashed against judicial officers, the very backbone of civil society. During the forced closure of the courts, George was determined to document and uphold the cases that remained unheard, but when armed groups threatened his life, he realized just how fragile the rule of law had become. He reveals how many of his colleagues fled, leaving him to carry the burden of ensuring justice was not completely abandoned. With heavy emotions, he narrates the pain of watching citizens turn increasingly desperate, their cases swallowed by a justice vacuum fueled by fear and uncertainty. His harrowing experiences have transformed him into a chronicler of injustice, one who not only bears witness but also urges the international community to consider the ramifications of silence.

Yet, in the turmoil, resilience was present, as demonstrated in the stories of community-based activists like Samuel, who partnered with legal practitioners to create a network aimed at offering resources for individuals desperate for legal representation. Samuel became the eyes and ears on the ground, gathering testimonies from victims in a region where voices had been stifled for far too long. He outlined the case of a widowed mother who had lost her husband in an incident involving armed forces. Their home was ransacked, and Samuel, seeing the injustice unfold, knew he had to act. He collaborated with local lawyers to organize community meetings, helping victims articulate their grievances and redirecting their anger towards pursuing legal channels. The sheer act of creating a space for individuals to express their pain often proved therapeutic, uniting them in solidarity against a common foe. Samuel celebrated those moments when the community gathered to confront their oppressors, showing them the constitution that had once been a promise of protection—testimonies forming a rallying cry for change.

As this stand-off with the law continued, some lawyers sought refuge in international platforms, attempting to shine a spotlight on the atrocities occurring in their homeland.

Fiona, an international relations attorney, took her campaign for justice beyond Cameroonian borders, advocating for awareness and support from non-governmental organizations. Through a series of interviews with media outlets, she developed a narrative that captured the plight of her compatriots—a harrowing blend of the personal and the political that resonated with international audiences. Fiona's story arguably becomes one of hope and heartbreak. Her relentless push for justice led her to testify before international bodies, detailing the experiences of her fellow lawyers and citizens suffering under an oppressive regime. Despite facing threats from both governmental and separatist entities, Fiona remained determined to lend her voice to the voiceless. As she elaborated on cases of torture and disappearances, she developed relationships with foreign correspondents, effectively turning her story into a global narrative aimed at energizing advocacy efforts worldwide. Her unwavering determination served as an inspiration to others who felt relinquished in the eyes of a broken system.

The sub-chapter of case studies serves as a tapestry woven from the threads of suffering and resilience, illustrating the immense toll that the Anglophone crisis has taken on those who uphold justice in the conflict setting. It encapsulates the stories of individuals navigating through fear, despair, and a relentless pursuit of righteousness, emphasizing that even in the darkest hour, there shines a flicker of hope—each testimony revealing not only the gravity of judicial failures but the irrevocable human spirit fighting for what is inherently just. Through these narratives, the reader is invited into the lives of individuals who, despite surrounding chaos, remain unyielding advocates of justice, illuminating the critical need for societal and institutional reforms in the wake of an ever-spiraling crisis. They remind us that justice is not a privilege, but a fundamental right that must be defended against the very conflicts that seek to erode its foundation.

Chapter 4:

Impact on Legal Proceedings

4.1 Delays in Justice

In the shadow of the Anglophone crisis, the legal proceedings in Cameroon's English-speaking regions have not only experienced excruciating delays but also a dramatic shift in the mechanisms that facilitate justice, which have left countless citizens stranded in a labyrinth of uncertainty and despair. At the heart of this tragedy are a myriad of factors converging to create an environment where justice is not an attainable right but a bitter mirage that continues to evade the grasp of those in distress.

The first layer of this unsettling tapestry is the simple and cruel reality of violence. The clashing forces have led to palpable disruptions in court operations, with judicial officers displaced, court buildings ransacked, and the entire legal infrastructure effectively dismantled. When the very pillars of the judicial system are threatened, the course of justice is inevitably disrupted, resulting in interminable delays.

Moreover, the role of legal practitioners, once the defenders of the law, has undergone a significant reconfiguration. Many lawyers have found themselves not only unable to access the courts due to safety concerns but are themselves targets of intimidation, leaving them paralyzed and unwilling to represent those who need them most. With an atmosphere steeped in fear and uncertainty, the absence of legal representation becomes a formidable barrier. Litigants, whether victims of crimes or individuals seeking restitution, often arrive at court only to discover that their lawyers are either absent, unprepared, or navigating their own crises. The erosion of trust in the very system designed to provide recourse has made many individuals hesitant to pursue claims, as they fear that the absence of legal backing will render their voices mute.

The delays are exacerbated by the sheer number of unresolved cases that have piled up, akin to a dam on the verge of breaking, which has led to a significant backlog in legal proceedings. Courts that once operated on a schedule find themselves operating sporadically, dragging their feet amid fears of violence and chaos, creating an exodus not just of judicial officers but also of the very citizens whom the judicial system was meant to serve. Individuals who, under normal circumstances, would have access to timely hearings and resolution of their legal matters now find themselves languishing in uncertainty as months turn into years, with little recourse or hope of resolution. Each delay represents a painful story of a life put on hold, of rights unrecognized, and of injustices that fester while the courts remain silent.

This quest for justice in the midst of disarray raises pressing questions about the implications of such delays on human rights. In environments where the rule of law is diminished, individuals become increasingly vulnerable to violations of their rights—arbitrary detention, unlawful imprisonment, and even torture. As the backlog of cases increases, the chances of fair trial rights being eroded becomes a stark reality. The principle of a speedy trial, enshrined as a fundamental human right in legal instruments, morphs into an abstract concept in the Anglophone context, with countless individuals being denied their most basic rights. The longer these cases remain unresolved, the more marginalized these individuals become, perpetually awaiting justice that never arrives.

The psychological toll is equally profound and paralyzing. Individuals waiting for justice to be served can be driven to despair, creating a cycle of hopelessness that can be nearly impossible to escape from. It is a suffocating experience that often leads to loss of faith in the legal system—ironically the very institution meant to uphold their dignity and rights. Cases of individuals who, despite overwhelming evidence, find themselves mired in unending bureaucratic limbo only serve to magnify the failure of the legal system. The anguish of parents waiting for the resolution of cases involving their children, or victims yearning for acknowledgment of their suffering, paints a picture of a society gripped by a perverse sense of impotence.

Compounding this is the physical and logistical inability of courts to process cases in a timely manner in the midst of the ongoing disruptions, compounded by the scarcity of resources dedicated to legal aid. Organizations formerly aiding the disenfranchised are struggling to maintain their operations when their own safety is in question, leading to additional delays. Many victims are unaware of their rights or lack the necessary information on how to navigate this fractured system effectively. Those without resources, connections, or knowledge about legal mechanisms are, in effect, silenced. The lack of public engagement and awareness surrounding the ongoing crisis only amplifies this sense of abandonment, wherein citizens suffer in silence, unaware that there is still a fight to be fought for their rights.

Yet in this disarray, stories of resilience emerge, underscoring the human spirit's tenacity in seeking resolution against all odds. Some legal practitioners continue to labor in the trenches, advocating for those who have been left behind, their commitment undeterred even as the challenges mount. Community-based initiatives, albeit constrained, are mobilizing to address the burgeoning crisis, attempting to adjust to the reality of the situation through informal mediation or legal workshops aimed at empowering individuals who might otherwise remain powerless. These community efforts exemplify the adaptive capacities of civil society, where ordinary citizens are stepping beyond their comfort zones to reclaim a semblance of agency and legality amid the chaos.

The urgency of reforming the justice system in the Anglophone regions has never been clearer. As the cries of citizens waiting for justice grow louder, a cumulative responsibility emerges for legal practitioners, policymakers, and international observers alike. Efforts must be coordinated not only to restore the judiciary's functionality but to rebuild the public's faith in a system that has, for far too long, now remained dormant. Innovations and external support must be conceptualized, exploring pathways to expedite the resolution of pending cases and ensuring individuals have access to essential legal resources and representation. By placing a renewed emphasis on the rights of individuals awaiting due process, society will not only restore the fabric of justice but also reaffirm its commitment to upholding the very ideals that underpin its democratic ethos. The path to justice might be fraught with challenges, but collectively it lies within the resolve to confront the delays with urgency, to advocate for change, and to reinforce the notion that justice, even in the tumult of crisis, must find a way to prevail.

4.2 Absence of Representation

The absence of legal representation in the Anglophone regions of Cameroon has emerged as one of the most alarming consequences of the ongoing crisis, profoundly impacting victims of violence and injustice. As the conflict has deepened, the court systems, which serve as the backbone of the judiciary, have seen an unprecedented erosion of their capacity to afford individuals the representation necessary to secure fair trials. With court houses destroyed, judges displaced, and legal practitioners fleeing due to intimidation or violence, countless citizens remain stranded in a limbo where their rights are threatened and often unrecognized. For those caught in this cycle, the absence of representation translates into a broader disregard for due process, where legal procedures become mere vestiges of a functioning judicial framework.

In an environment stripped of effective legal counsel, the plight of victims who seek justice becomes fraught with insurmountable challenges. Families of those arbitrarily detained or victims of violent crimes often find themselves standing alone, grappling with the complexities of a justice system that has all but collapsed. Without the guiding hand of a lawyer, these individuals face not only the devastating emotional toll of their circumstances but a legal landscape that is perplexingly navigable only through previous experience or sheer luck. If there was ever a time where victims needed advocates—individuals skilled in the art of legal intricacies—this is unequivocally the moment, yet those advocates have been pushed to the fringes or entirely out of reach, leaving their clients vulnerable and exposed.

Delays have become the modus operandi of the courts where they continue to operate, and the lack of representation only exacerbates the situation. Procedural delays, insufficient resources, and an overwhelming backlog of cases mean that victims waiting for their day in court often feel forgotten, their pleas drowned out by bureaucratic inertia. In many instances, these delays become so protracted that witnesses lose their relevance, evidence degrades, and the fundamental right to a timely trial dissipates into the ether of a compromised legal system. In the absence of counsel, the ramifications of such inertia are magnified—the lack of proper legal representation means that even when victims are finally granted their moment in court, they step into a minefield without the necessary tools to navigate their claims. The intricacies of law remain shrouded in mystery for those who are not educated in legal matters; thus, the right to a fair trial begins to take on the form of an illusion, blending into the reality of coercion and inequality.

Stories abound of desperate individuals turning to unofficial channels for advice, often from families or friends who themselves lack the knowledge and expertise to provide meaningful guidance. As misinformation proliferates, many victims of crime find themselves misled, having made legal decisions based on half-truths or misconceptions. This not only leads to further legal entanglements but also emboldens unscrupulous actors who prey on the vulnerable, offering services that may hold the allure of resolution while remaining devoid of the integrity of established legal practices. Thus, the absence of formal legal representation does not merely inhibit access to justice; it exacerbates a greater crisis of legality and legitimacy, creating a disillusioning feedback loop that further entrenches inequality and despair.

As the legal framework of the Anglophone regions crumbles, numerous NGOs and civil society organizations (CSOs) have made resilient attempts to fill the representation void, albeit with their own set of challenges. While these organizations often serve as lifelines, providing legal advice and support to those unable to obtain traditional legal representation, they are neither a panacea nor sustainable solutions in the long run. These entities operate under immense pressure, with limited funding, and often face the dual threats of intimidation from state actors and dilemmas posed by the prevailing conflict. Many legal practitioners who choose to align with these organizations do so at great personal risk, encountering hostility from both the government and armed groups alike. The atmosphere of fear and distrust erodes the very fabric of advocacy, creating additional barriers that impede the operation of these admirable efforts to restore agency to victims.

Access to justice is not merely a formal legal right; it is a lived experience, a fundamental human right that, when denied, lays the very groundwork for a culture of impunity permeating society. The absence of legal representation extends beyond individual cases but also stagnates societal progress and democratic ideals, turning victims into mere statistics within a context devoid of tangible action. When advocacy remains ineffective and legal representation unattainable, entire communities become unable to hold the perpetrators of violence accountable. The implications for social cohesion are dire, as mistrust takes root, provoking resentment against authorities and law enforcement while causing citizens to oscillate between silence and desperation. This breeds an environment wherein justice is perceived as an inaccessible ideal, further propagating the narrative that the legal system stands indifferent to the very individuals it is designed to protect.

As this crisis continues to unfold, calls for reform grow louder; however, the urgency for action transcends policy discussions—it requires a recognition of the fundamental human experiences marred by the absence of representation. Empowering victims means recognizing the inherent dignity of each individual seeking redress and ensuring that those who have experienced trauma receive comprehensive legal support. The challenge rests with both the government and civil society, advocating in unison not only for systematic changes but for the restoration of the trust that has been eroded in the midst of this nightmare.

In the Anglophone regions of Cameroon, the absence of legal representation is a clarion call for social justice, demanding a unified response that prioritizes the restoration of legal frameworks and the rights of victims. Achieving this goal will not be easy—historical patterns of neglect and marginalization must be dismantled, necessitating a coordinated effort from all stakeholders. Yet, it is only through recognizing the hardships faced by the populace, the relentless struggles against an indifferent or hostile system, and the plight of individuals trapped without legal counsel, that one can hope to instigate the necessary transformations. Ultimately, the challenge of restoring representation is tantamount to reclaiming the very foundation of justice itself, reaffirming the realities that law exists not in theory but as an active, lived experience that shapes and uplifts communities. A future built on justice, equality, and respect for human rights can only emerge from the ashes of a crumbling legal system if those who have the power to effect change act urgently and decisively within the troubled landscape of the Anglophone crisis.

4.3 Erosion of Fair Trial Rights

In the tumultuous landscape of the Anglophone crisis, where every corner of daily life is marred by conflict, the principles of fair trial rights have suffered grievous erosion. The very framework designed to uphold justice has been systematically undermined, rendering the aspirations of many for equitable legal recourse distant and largely unattainable. Within this disrupted environment, profound delays in legal proceedings have become commonplace. Faced with the harrowing realities of ongoing violence and instability, courts have frequently ceased to operate, or, when they do, they confront overwhelming backlogs. This paralysis delays judicial processes for thousands of litigants who, in different circumstances, would be granted timely access to their day in court. The consequence of these delays is not merely a frustrating waiting period; they symbolize the denial of justice, effectively extinguishing the hope of resolution for many individuals caught in a web of unresolved grievances.

The nature of these delays is compounded by the alarming absence of legal representation. In effect, the conflict has created a situation in which access to professional legal assistance is not just limited, but often entirely out of reach, particularly for marginalized groups who lack both resources and connections. The few practicing lawyers within the Anglophone regions find themselves under siege, navigating not only the physical dangers presented by the ongoing violence but also the increasingly oppressive climate of intimidation directed at legal practitioners. Many lawyers have left the area entirely, either seeking safety elsewhere or paralyzed by a sense of helplessness in the face of a judiciary rendered impotent due to the upheaval. Those who remain often do so at great peril, forced to balance their commitment to justice with the instinct for self-preservation. In many cases, individuals requiring legal representation are left to fend for themselves, lacking the necessary skills or knowledge to effectively advocate for their rights within a deeply flawed and hostile legal system. Not only does this situation reflect a colossal injustice it as well enforces a pervasive feeling of abandonment among citizens, who watch as their rights evaporate under the glare of conflict and chaos.

The erosion of fair trial rights also extends into the very operations of the judiciary itself. Structures meant to uphold the sanctity of the legal process have been dismantled or repurposed, disrupted by violence and the detainment of judicial officers who have fallen victim to either displacement or outright aggression. The courtrooms, once hallowed spaces where the machinations of justice could unfold, have, in many instances, become mere shells of their former selves. Security concerns have left them vulnerable, while the lack of resources and personnel has diminished their ability to function in accordance with established legal standards. As a result, the trials that do occur are increasingly characterized by arbitrariness, devoid of the due process guarantees that define a fair trial. Litigants find themselves navigating an uncharted terrain, where the truth is often eclipsed by the chaos of violence, and legal determinations may hinge on extrajudicial factors rather than solid evidence or sound legal arguments. The fundamental rights to be heard, to produce evidence, and to argue one's case in an impartial setting have been systematically eroded, creating a chasm between the ideals of justice and the grim reality experienced by those embroiled in legal battles.

Furthermore, the suppression of dissenting voices within the judicial sector contributes to this alarming deterioration of fair trial standards. Legal practitioners and judges who dare to speak out against the injustices perpetrated during the conflict often find themselves subjected to harassment, threats, or worse. This environment of fear inhibits the independence of the judiciary and fosters a culture of silence that further compromises the integrity of legal proceedings. The rising tide of self-censorship among legal professionals only deepens the crisis, as even those who wish to defend the rights of the marginalized may hesitate to act, fearing for their own safety. The pervasive climate of intimidation has rendered the justice system a shadow of what it ought to be—a reliable mechanism for resolving disputes and advocating for the rights of citizens. One can hardly expect the courts to function with fairness and equity when those tasked with upholding justice operate under constant threat, unable or unwilling to challenge the prevailing forces of oppression and arbitrariness.

As we dissect the fabric of fair trial principles that is tragically unraveling in the context of the Anglophone crisis, it becomes increasingly clear that solutions are urgently needed. A comprehensive approach to restore the rule of law must encompass enhancing the security and independence of the judiciary, ensuring that legal practitioners can operate free from duress, while simultaneously establishing frameworks that make legal representation accessible to all. Dialogues among stakeholders—including civil society organizations, legal associations, and humanitarian groups—are essential in charting a path toward revitalizing the justice sector, focusing on the restoration of a credible and functioning judiciary as a pivotal element for peace and reconciliation. Equal access to justice must be elevated as a priority, underscoring the importance of resilient legal frameworks that can withstand the pressures of conflict. Empowering communities by providing legal education and resources will not only help individuals navigate the complexities of their legal rights but also foster broader societal engagement in the quest for accountability and justice.

The deterioration of fair trial rights during the Anglophone crisis serves as a stark reminder of the fragility of justice systems in times of conflict. It reflects a devastating intersection where debilitating poverty and systemic oppression converge with the aspirations of citizens yearning for equity. It is a moment pregnant with potential change, not just for those embroiled in the crisis, but for the future of justice in Cameroon as a whole. As we reflect on the personal stories interwoven throughout this narrative, we cannot ignore the urgent call to action that emerges from the ashes of this struggle. It is only through collective efforts that we might begin to weave together the frayed threads of community resilience, judicial independence, and the enduring promise of fair trials—a commitment to justice that must remain steadfast even when it lies in the crossfire of conflict.

Chapter 5:

Destruction of Court Infrastructure

5.1 Physical Damage

The physical damage to court facilities in the Anglophone regions of Cameroon stands as a harrowing testament to the relentless conflict that has engulfed these areas. What were once symbols of justice and the rule of law have been reduced to mere shells of their former selves, unveiling a narrative of despair, displacement, and disillusionment. The very infrastructure that sustained legal proceedings now lays in ruins, a reflection of the broader societal collapse engendered by the strife between governmental forces and separatist factions. As we sift through the debris left behind, we become acutely aware of the indelible scars etched into both the buildings and the lives of the people who once sought solace within their walls.

In notable towns like Batibo, Tombel, and Limbe, amongst others, the remnants of court buildings evoke a sense of loss not just for the judiciary but for social order itself. The once austere facades, which exuded strength and reliability, have been shattered by indiscriminate gunfire and purposeful destruction, leaving windows gaping like open wounds. In many instances, entire courthouses have been set ablaze, the fires mirroring the rage of a populace caught in the turmoil of an unrelenting struggle for autonomy. This destruction strikes at the heart of the legal framework; courts, as the bastions of justice, lay uninhabitable, and the judicial processes upon which the lives of many depended ground to an abrupt halt. Legal practitioners, judges, and citizens alike have been left scrambling in an environment where the mere act of seeking justice has become fraught with peril.

Within this morass of destruction, the loss of physical resources compounds the travails faced by the justice system. Libraries once rife with legal texts, precedents, and essential documentation have been severely compromised or entirely obliterated. The essential tools that equipped legal practitioners to navigate the complex landscape of Cameroonian law are now nothing but scattered pages with the remains of what were once invaluable assets. In a region already grappling with gains made in legal education and advocacy, this loss translates into a significant setback. Without access to vital legal resources, the ability to train emerging lawyers or to provide robust defense becomes an increasingly Sisyphean task. The fledgling hope of bolstering a system mired in uncertainty now hangs in the balance, further stifled by the absence of a functioning judiciary.

As the very architecture designed to protect rights and administer equity crumbles, the human ramifications are profound and multifaceted. Individuals who desperately sought legal redress find themselves adrift, unable to access the justice system when they need it most. Litigants find themselves bereft of the means to file cases or attend hearings because their local court has either been destroyed or rendered inaccessible due to ongoing violence. The verdicts on their grievances are delayed indefinitely, and with each passing day, the stakes escalate. Accusations linger in the wind without the forum for recourse, and the anxieties borne from the uncertainty of one's future become a persistent companion. As the common saying goes, justice delayed is justice denied, and in this unfolding crisis, those who wish to assert their rights are met with barriers that seem insurmountable, thrusting them into a state of utter despair.

The breakdown of court physicality has further repercussions beyond mere accessibility. The fear that has seeped into the judicial process reshapes the societal understanding of justice itself. Once viewed as a reliable cardinal principle, the concept of justice now morphs into a ghostly vision, one that looms large over communities but feels increasingly unattainable. The loss of a functional court system degrades the trust between the citizens and their institutions. People begin to internalize the notion that the law is impotent, engendering a culture of silence and submission among those who might otherwise have sought to assert their rights. In many ways, the destruction of legal structures serves as a broader metaphor for the erosion of hope, as individuals grapple with an existential crisis: convinced that the laws that govern them are no longer applicable in the prevailing chaos.

Further complicating this untenable situation is the displacement of judicial officers from their locales. Many judges and lawyers have fled their posts out of fear for their lives, thus exacerbating the justice vacuum. The absence of these officers, who are skillfully trained to navigate legal complexities and act as impartial arbiters, leaves communities without the mediation necessary to resolve disputes. Widespread displacement of the judicial workforce hampers not only the courts themselves but also the essential projects aimed at legal education and community engagement. Those who might have taken up positions in courts find themselves unable to fulfill basic responsibilities, and as a direct consequence, countless cases remain unresolved. This state of paralysis underlines a fundamental truth—the law is an unwavering pillar for societal cohesion, and its destruction elicits a ripple effect far beyond its physical manifestations.

The palpable despair emerging from the destruction of court facilities is a story shared by many—judges, lawyers, and litigants alike. They recount their experiences with aching clarity, their eyes shimmering with memories of the bustling corridors that once echoed with deliberations and legal proceedings. A judicial officer may recall the laughter of clerks and the stirring debates between opposing counsel, all now replaced by haunting silence. A lawyer may find it difficult to suppress tears while reflecting on the dreams of creating a just society, now shattered by the harsh realities of a broken system. Each testimony reveals the indelible connection between physical spaces and the emotional landscapes they hold, illuminating the extent to which the damage inflicted upon courthouses reverberates throughout society itself.

In light of the physical and emotional devastation inflicted upon the legal framework in the Anglophone regions of Cameroon, one cannot overlook the urgent need for healing and restoration. Advocacy for rebuilding must not only center on restoring infrastructures but also focus on re-establishing trust within communities. Engagement strategies must involve the voices of the victims and include wide-ranging consultations with those directly impacted by the conflict. The return to legal normalcy hinges on an inclusive and participatory process, one that seeks to revive that which has been lost while addressing the gaping wounds festering within the societal fabric.

The journey toward reconstruction will demand both resilience and advocacy to repurpose abandoned spaces into loci of justice, places where the law once again finds expression. The physical restoration of the courts will necessitate a concerted effort from all corners—government, civil society, and international partners—collaborating to develop a vision for a revitalized judicial system that bears the marks of its trials yet rises anew with fortified purpose. Within this framework, the narratives of pain can connect to streams of hope, giving rise to a future where the merits of access to justice ring true for every citizen, paving pathways toward meaningful dialogues, reconciliation, and long-lasting peace. The reconstruction of court facilities is only the first step in the process and it is merely physical space we must reclaim, along with the values, trust, and faith in justice upheld therein. The road ahead is long and fraught with challenges, but it is a journey that must be traversed if the promise of justice is to endure in the face of adversity.

5.2 Loss of Resources

As the air thickened with tension and uncertainty in the Anglophone regions of Cameroon, the loss of legal resources became painfully apparent. This deterioration stretched beyond mere infrastructure: it epitomized a systemic collapse that crippled the very foundations of justice. Court buildings, once towering symbols of order and stability within communities, were reduced to rubble, standing as testament to a conflict that redefined the notion of safety and sanctuary. Destruction did not solely target physical structures; it tore through the veins of a legal ecosystem, leaving behind a trail of despair where the practice of law was once vibrant and meaningful. The impact of this destruction resonated far and wide, reaching those who sought justice as well as those whose mandates were to deliver it.

Across the regions enveloped in turmoil, courthouse landscapes were marked by charred remains and shattered glass. These buildings had been the forum and the final bastion for countless cases—family disputes, criminal prosecutions, civil matters—all interwoven with the quotidian lives of the citizens. With their obliteration, the belief in a legal system dedicated to fairness and equity was shaken to its core. An unidentifiable silence enveloped the squares that once thrummed with the ebbs and flows of judicial proceedings, replaced now by an eerie stillness that spoke volumes of lost hope. Legal practitioners became refugees in their homeland, displaced from the very institutions that empowered them to uphold the law. Judges, lawyers, court clerks, and administrative staff were severed from their roles, swirling into the vortex of vulnerability that the conflict unleashed. Many of them sought refuge across borders or within other regions, carrying with them not only their personal belongings but also the weight of memories—a legacy of dedication to justice now overshadowed by personal trauma and uncertainty.

As the legal professionals scattered, the void left by their absence sent ripples through communities that had long relied on their expertise and guidance. Ordinary citizens found themselves trapped in a bureaucratic limbo, with the routes to legal recourse either completely obliterated or rendered unapproachable due to safety concerns. Court cases languished, unresolved and unattended, creating a backlog that suffocated the concept of due process. With each passing day, the barriers to accessing justice grew higher, escalating the sense of despair among those searching for answers to their grievances. Vulnerable individuals and marginalized groups, already at risk in such tumultuous environments, faced unprecedented obstacles in asserting their rights. The law, which should serve as a shield against arbitrary actions, became an inaccessible fortress, leaving many to suffer in silence.

The evisceration of judicial resources was compounded by the hostile environment that developed in the conflict. Many lawyers who brave the conflict to continue their practice find themselves facing threats and harassment, a dangerous game of cat and mouse where the stakes are their lives. The intimidation seeped into the fabric of the legal community, chilling the zeal for advocacy and creating a phenomenon wherein even the most tenacious legal minds hesitated to step foot into the underbelly of the beleaguered system. The long-standing tradition of camaraderie and mutual support among lawyers eroded, replaced by a survival-of-the-fittest mentality that further splintered the legal community. As the atmosphere crackled with danger, legal practitioners find themselves at an impasse: to defend the rights of their clients meant risking their well-being, and to remain silent was to acquiesce to the very injustices that they had vowed to combat.

Laid bare, the loss of resources encapsulates not just bricks and mortar but also the very principles that underpin a functioning democracy. Access to justice, equal representation, and the right to a fair hearing becomes a battleground marked by pain and disillusionment. Policies that could once depend on legal frameworks crumbled, leaving behind a disjointed, and ignored environment where the vulnerabilities of individuals were exploited. Law enforcement agencies struggled to meet the need for justice, marred by the imperfections of a broken system. The forfeiture of legal resources impacted not only the prosecution of crimes but also the mechanisms of accountability that should have been the bulwark against state excesses. As citizens roam the streets, their fears grow not only from the violence of the conflict but from a burgeoning realization that the law has become as much a weapon against them as a source of protection.

In the chaos, the resilience of communities shone through. Grassroots organizations emerged from the wreckage, striving to create alternative forms of humanitarian and legal assistance as a means of bridging the lacunae left by the void in the formal legal system. Lawyers often formed coalitions with non-governmental organizations to set up temporary legal aid clinics and mobile courts, acting as lifelines for those who felt hopeless. However, such efforts were often fraught with their own challenges, as the coalitions faced scant resources and an uphill battle to foster trust within communities that had witnessed firsthand the inadequacies of institutions designed to serve them.

The existing pathways to reinstate the legal resources and personnel seemed daunting and labyrinthine. A collaborative approach, involving stakeholders at all levels—from policymakers and civil society to international bodies—is imperative for reviving the sense of agency that had been stripped away. Discussions around the reconstruction of court infrastructure often fell flat without acknowledging the systemic issues at play; any attempt at rebuilding the judiciary had to concurrently involve addressing the trauma experienced by both legal practitioners and the citizenry. Incremental steps could not suffice; it required the development of a sustainable framework that struck at the heart of rebuilding trust in a system that had betrayed its own.

As the Anglophone crisis continued to evolve, the incorporation of local narratives and experiences became increasingly essential in shaping the future of justice in the region. The voices of judicial officers, lawyers, and litigants needed to inform discussions on legal reform and resource allocation. Amplifying these personal stories created a tapestry of truth that would challenge policymakers to confront the grim reality of lost resources. The urgency for solutions could no longer be relegated to the peripheries of political discourse; it demanded immediate attention, fostering a collective responsibility among stakeholders to re-imagine and reinforce the role of the judiciary as a cornerstone of society.

Thus, the story of loss morphed into a rallying cry for healing. The Anglophone crisis has illustrated unmistakably that justice cannot exist within a vacuum, nor can it thrive in the midst of fear and chaos. The robust legal traditions that once bolstered communities' ability to defend their rights must not only be restored but also redefined to ensure future resilience. Each day that passed without the rectification of the devastating losses experienced only exacerbated the ramifications. A renewed commitment from all corners of society is critical, driven by the understanding that a functioning judiciary was not merely an abstract concept but a fundamental human right—a right that must be championed vigorously, both in times of peace and in the most harrowing conflicts. The journey to rebuild the legal system in Cameroon's Anglophone regions would be arduous and tested by ongoing strife, yet it also served as an avenue for realigning values around justice, dignity, and respect—values that had been too long eclipsed by the shadows of strife.

5.3 Long-term Consequences

The long-term consequences of the destruction of courthouses and the dismantling of legal infrastructure in the Anglophone regions of Cameroon are profound and multifaceted, threatening not only the fabric of the legal system but also the very essence of societal stability and community trust. As court buildings lay in ruins, their physical remnants serve as stark symbols of a judicial system in disarray, undermining the rule of law and jeopardizing the fundamental rights of citizens. The obliteration of these legal institutions erodes the sense of security that citizens derive from a functional judiciary. Access to justice becomes a mere illusion, and the dis-empowerment felt by ordinary citizens is palpable. The absence of courts spells disaster for the principle of accountability, as individuals emboldened by impunity wreak havoc, knowing that their actions are unlikely to face legal repercussions. Without the judiciary as a check on power, both state and non-state actors may exploit the vacuum, leading to a further descent into lawlessness.

Moreover, the displacement of judges and legal personnel exacerbates the crisis. When judicial officials are forced into exile or abandon their posts out of fear for their safety, the knowledgeable guardians of the law become scarce commodities. This shortage is not merely a matter of numbers but it also robs the system of the critical expertise and moral authority necessary to uphold justice in a tumultuous environment. As a result, even the mere logistics of legal proceedings face staggering challenges. Cases linger unresolved, legal representation becomes sporadic, and the confidence of communities in seeking justice diminishes. Furthermore, the psychological toll on those who have previously dedicated their lives to the law cannot be overstated. Judges, lawyers, and court clerks who have been displaced are left grappling with feelings of inadequacy and helplessness. Their training and years of practice rendered obsolete in the presence of chaos and violence create a gap not just in legal knowledge but also in the human touch necessary for adjudication. The deterioration of the legal profession in such a manner breeds a cynicism among those who remain, who may question the efficacy of their work within a backdrop of conflict and fear.

Communities are also deeply affected by these developments. The justice system traditionally served as a symbol of societal cohesion, where grievances could be resolved in a structured manner. The erosion of this structure lays bare fractures within communities and fosters an environment ripe for conflict. When the pathways to dispute resolution are blocked, estrangements grow and relationships suffer. As individuals resort to self-help and alternative dispute resolution methods—often steeped in cultural practices that lack fair representation—the potential for violence escalates, as the legitimacy of authorities fades. The broader implications extend beyond immediate fracturing; the collective trust in communal norms and the social contract deteriorates, resulting in disillusionment and further societal rifts. Youth who grow up witnessing this breakdown of order may adopt a pervasive distrust of the rule of law, creating a cycle of violence and instability that perpetuates itself across generations.

Furthermore, the long-term economic implications of this breakdown in the judicial framework cannot be ignored. A functional justice system underpins economic stability, as it provides the assurance that contracts will be honored, businesses protected, and property rights safeguarded. With the chaos wrought by the Anglophone crisis leading to the closure or destruction of courts, the investment climate drastically shifts, sidelining potential investors wary of conducting transactions in an environment devoid of legal recourse. Entrepreneurs, especially those in the informal sector, face increased risks of exploitation, theft, and arbitrary evictions without the safety net that formal legal systems are intended to provide. This destabilization reverberates through the economy, leading to broader issues of poverty and underdevelopment, where communities struggle to forge ahead as their aspirations are stifled by an absence of justice.

The fragmentation of the legal system further endangers human rights, creating an environment in which abuses can flourish with little oversight or recourse. In the absence of courts to provide redress, victims of human rights violations, including unlawful detentions, torture, and extrajudicial killings, find themselves with no avenues for justice. The disintegration of legal protections foments a culture of impunity, emboldening both state and non-state actors to infringe upon rights without the fear of accountability. The continuing cycle of violence and vindication of abuses not only causes immediate harm but also sows the seeds for societal trauma, imprinting scars that often take generations to heal. The long-term psychological consequences on individuals and communities can manifest in various forms, including increased anxiety, vulnerability to addiction, and fragmentation of social bonds, leading to a pervasive sense of hopelessness and despair that may transmute into active resistance or rebellion.

Many civic organizations and NGOs, essential players in advocating for justice and human rights, also suffer as a consequence of this ongoing turmoil. Funding can dry up, owing to shifting priorities away from international attention, granted to the newsworthy conflicts, but without sustained commitment to rebuilding of civil society. As the courtroom doors remain closed, alternative forms of advocacy become increasingly strained; the voices of those they aim to uplift are lost in the noise of an unrelenting crisis, while their own operational capacity is eroded due to the ongoing conflict. This absence of external support and advocacy means that the plight of citizens becomes invisible on international platforms, and critical conversations surrounding human rights can fray further due to an almost audible silence from those who would otherwise speak for the marginalized.

Entering the stage of peace-building, the idea of reconciliation pivots yet again on the availability and functionality of a competent judiciary. After conflict, societies must reckon with their pasts, and the mechanisms of justice must play pivotal roles in creating space for dialogue and forgiveness. However, the absence of a stable judicial framework complicates transitional justice efforts that aim to address grievances, provide restitution, and forge renewed social contracts. The capacity for restorative principles, whereby communities learn and heal in the shadow of shared understandings, diminishes alongside judicial authority. This challenges transitional leaderships and peace processes equally, rendering them less effective at building sustainable peace.

The path forward seems daunting, but it is crucial to focus not only on the psychosocial repair of hijacked judicial systems but also their reintegration into the larger paradigm of civic life and community evolution. The response to the Anglophone crisis must embrace resilience rather than despair. People and institutions need encouragement to rebuild, to reclaim the authority that has been lost, to restore the rhythm of a society where justice is not merely an abstract principle but a lived reality. Thus, the long-term implications of the crisis extend far beyond the immediate damage done to buildings. They penetrate deep into the psyche of citizens, the fabric of community norms, the landscape of economic ambition, and the core of fundamental rights and liberties. Only by recognizing and addressing these cascading effects can generations hope to reclaim space for justice, autonomy, and ultimately, a renewed belief in the potential for a flourishing society beyond the confines of trauma.

Chapter 6:

The Role of Civil Society

6.1 Legal Aid Initiatives

In the midst of the Anglophone crisis in Cameroon, a concerted effort by various NGOs and community organizations has focused on providing legal aid and support to the victims profoundly affected by the disruption to the judiciary. These initiatives have become lifelines for individuals caught in a quagmire of injustice, where the legal system, once a beacon of hope, has been reduced to shadows of its former self. The derailment of law and order, a direct consequence of violent conflict, left countless citizens bereft of the protections that come with access to justice. In response, numerous humanitarian organizations have mobilized, striving to fill the void where the state has faltered, emphasizing the necessity for legal representation and assistance.

One of the primary ventures undertaken by these NGOs involves the establishment of mobile legal clinics that traverse the conflict-affected areas. These clinics are fundamental in reaching out to individuals who have been displaced or cannot access traditional court systems due to safety concerns. By deploying trained legal practitioners into the heart of affected communities, they offer legal consultations, workshops, and simplified access to legal documents. This proactive approach not only serves to demystify the legal process but also endeavors to empower individuals with knowledge about their rights in times of crisis. Facilitating discussions about human rights and the legal recourse available has become a cornerstone of these initiatives, as many victims remain unaware of the avenues open to them for seeking justice.

Alongside mobile clinics, partnerships have emerged with local law schools to utilize the skills of students and professors who are eager to contribute to the humanitarian cause. These partnerships stimulate a rich environment for both learning and advocacy, as students gain practical experience while assisting clients in preparing their cases and understanding judicial proceedings. The exchange is mutually beneficial, fostering a generation of future lawyers who are not only skilled in their craft but are also socially conscious and aware of the glaring disparities within the justice system. Workshops designed for community leaders to enhance their understanding of legal rights have also become critical components, seeking to build a more informed citizenry capable of advocating for themselves and their peers.

The efforts of these organizations extend beyond immediate legal aid; they also promote advocacy for systematic reforms. They engage with policymakers and stakeholders, bringing their findings to the forefront in a bid to address the underlying issues that hinder access to justice. A notable example of such advocacy is the coalition formed by various NGOs and civil society organizations (CSOs) that aim to press for legislation that safeguards the independence of the judiciary and ensures a more robust system of legal aid, prioritizing victims' rights. By collecting testimonies and case studies from individuals directly affected by the conflict, they present compelling narratives to illustrate the urgency of their cause, ensuring that the voices of the marginalized are not overlooked in the corridors of power.

In addition to these structural initiatives, psychological support and holistic care have become increasingly recognized as vital elements of legal assistance. Many organizations have integrated psychological counseling into their services, acknowledging that the traumas of violence and displacement impact not just the legal plight of victims but their overall well-being. The shared experiences of suffering foster a sense of community, and support groups often form around these programs, allowing for collective healing and resilience. Legal aid is not merely a transactional interaction but it is also imbued with empathy, understanding, and the aim of restoring dignity to those who have been subjected to relentless adversity.

The narratives surrounding these legal aid initiatives illustrate the resilience of communities that rise within the turmoil to advocate for their own rights. Ordinary citizens, often underestimated, have mobilized as well, forming grassroots movements that push for reform and accountability. This synergy between grassroots and organized NGO efforts demonstrates a powerful communal response to injustice, characterized not only by a desire to access legal representation but to reshape the very foundations upon which justice is built. Ultimately, the initiatives aimed at providing legal assistance within the conflict-ridden Anglophone regions of Cameroon showcase the enduring spirit of the human endeavor even in the darkest of times, reminding us that justice, while obstructed, is a persistent pursuit that refuses to be extinguished. The hopes and aspirations woven through these stories become a testament to the possibility of change and the emergence of a more just society, where the mechanisms of legal recourse are not contingent upon one's geographical or socio-political circumstances.

6.2 Advocacy and Awareness

In the heart of the Anglophone crisis, advocacy and awareness efforts have emerged as vital lifelines for those caught in the throes of injustice. Various CSOs such as the Refugee Welfare Association Cameroon (REWAC), and other community organizations have stepped up, courageously working to illuminate the plight of individuals whose voices have been silenced by the chaos surrounding them. These organizations recognize that the fight for justice is not merely an abstract concept, but a palpable necessity that impacts the lives of countless civilians. With the absence of a robust legal system and the escalation of violence, these advocacy groups play a crucial role in bridging the gap between victims and the legal resources they desperately require. Their work is not just about providing legal aid, but also about fostering an environment where awareness of rights and legal protections can thrive, even amid turmoil.

As the conflict has unfolded, many CSOs have redirected their focus toward understanding the multifaceted nature of the Anglophone crisis. They have adopted comprehensive approaches, embedding themselves within the communities they serve, engaging locals to identify specific needs and mobilize resources effectively. Recognizing that conventional legal pathways have been significantly disrupted, these organizations have sought out alternative measures to provide support. Workshops and community meetings have become critical platforms for disseminating information on legal rights, enabling affected individuals to navigate their circumstances with a greater understanding of what justice entails. It is in these gatherings that personal stories are shared, breathing life into legal jargon, as individuals recount their harrowing experiences with the justice system—a system that has become inaccessible to many.

The challenges faced by those who seek justice in this conflict-ridden landscape are manifold, and advocacy groups have dedicated themselves to working directly with these individuals to alleviate some of the burdens. Front-line workers, often volunteers, are trained to offer guidance on how to document incidents of violence or discrimination, emphasizing the importance of evidence collection that could later support claims in court. The reality, however, is that many victims are often hesitant to speak out, fearing repercussions from armed groups or government forces. It is within this precarious context that CSOs emphasize the importance of confidentiality and protection for whistle blowers, creating safe spaces where victims can share their narratives without the threat of retaliation. Building trust becomes a foundational element of the work being done, as advocates earn the respect and confidence of those who have become all too wary of external intervention.

Simultaneously, CSOs have pursued broader public awareness campaigns to shine a light on the injustices inherent in the Anglophone crisis. Through strategic messaging on social media and traditional media outlets, these organizations have sought to inform a global audience about the plight of those affected. By documenting human rights violations and sharing compelling personal stories, they foster empathy and galvanize public support. The ability to rally international attention is vital, not only for securing funding and resources but also for applying pressure on governments and international bodies to respond to the situation. Advocacy is inherently a collective endeavor, and these organizations facilitate coalitions of stakeholders who are committed to restoring the rule of law and advancing human rights in the Anglophone regions.

The coupling of on-the-ground support with high-level advocacy highlights the effective synergy that can occur when community needs inform broader political dialogues. Hand-in-hand with legal empowerment initiatives, organizations have organized petitions, campaigns, and lobbying efforts directed at policymakers, urging them to take action and prioritize the protection of rights in regions suffering under conflict. These strategic interactions create a platform for victims to speak at events and forums, empowering them to tell their stories to influential actors who can influence change. This ripple effect of personal testimony reinforces the notion that advocacy is not a one-size-fits-all approach; rather, it must adapt to the local contexts and the particularities of the crises being faced.

Despite the progress made by advocacy groups, the road ahead is fraught with complexities. The legal landscape remains challenging, and the systemic obstacles imposed by conflict often overshadow individual efforts toward justice. These organizations regularly confront the limitations of existing legal frameworks, which are strained under the weight of the ongoing crisis. Nevertheless, activists remain undeterred. They continually strive to adapt their strategies, utilizing data-driven approaches to not only map the incidence of rights abuses but also to identify emerging trends. The insights gained from this research become instrumental in shaping both advocacy efforts and policy recommendations, emphasizing the need for robust legal systems that can withstand the shocks of conflict.

As they reflect on their work, many individuals involved in advocacy highlight the significance of community engagement in driving change. They understand that sustainable transformations often stem from grassroots involvement, where communities actively participate in defining their realities. Education, awareness, and mobilization are critical components of their strategy, as a well-informed populace is more apt to assert their rights and demand accountability. By weaving a narrative of resilience into their advocacy, community organizations inspire hope and remind individuals that the thirst for justice does not have to wither even in the face of overwhelming challenges. The stories are not just stories; they are evidence of humanity's enduring spirit, even amid adversity, capturing the essence of the collective struggle that defines the Anglophone experience.

Moreover, the technologies utilized by these organizations to maximize their outreach cannot be overstated. The proliferation of mobile technology has transformed how advocates connect with communities, allowing them to efficiently disseminate information and provide real-time responses to emerging threats. Text messaging and social media platforms have become vital tools for rapid communication, as advocates often use these channels to alert communities about potential dangers or updates on legal aid services. This integration of technology does not replace the personal touch required in advocacy but rather enhances traditional methods, enabling a more strategic approach to community engagement and information sharing.

The importance of mental health care within the advocacy framework has also emerged as a pivotal theme, as many survivors experience psychological trauma from their experiences. Organizations have begun to recognize that addressing the mental wellness of those impacted by conflict is integral to their path toward justice. By fostering access to therapeutic services and support networks, advocacy efforts can work holistically, emphasizing not only the need for legal representation but also the need to heal emotionally and psychologically.

This dual approach enhances the narrative of recovery for victims, bolstering their capacity to engage with the judicial process effectively.

In this unique landscape of advocacy, there are few clear victories, but each step forward offers a glimmer of hope. From the relentless efforts of CSOs and community organizations to the personal stories that drive these efforts, there exists a profound realization that though the law may falter, the human spirit remains unbroken. Through advocacy and awareness, there is an undeniable truth: as long as there are those willing to stand and fight for justice, there remains a semblance of hope—a belief that justice, though oftentimes elusive, is not beyond reach. As new generations rise, inspired by the narratives of struggle and resilience, the work of advocacy will continue to be pivotal in the discourse surrounding human rights, justice reform, and the restoration of rule of law in Cameroon. With unwavering dedication, these advocates lay the groundwork for a future where justice is not merely an ideal but a lived reality for every citizen in the Anglophone regions.

6.3 Challenges Faced

In the wake of the Anglophone crisis, civil society organizations have emerged as critical players in the battle for justice and human rights, tirelessly working to provide legal aid and support to victims caught in the maelstrom of conflict. However, the challenges they face are monumental, contoured by both the ongoing violence and the socio-political landscape that complicates their mission. Organizations dedicated to offering legal support find themselves navigating a treacherous path where the very rights they seek to uphold are constantly under siege. The multifaceted nature of this challenge creates a harsh environment, forcing these organizations to operate within a framework of duress that compromises their ability to function effectively. The personnel involved, often heroic in their conviction, must contend with the palpable fear that accompanies their work, lending a climate of intimidation to all endeavors aimed at promoting justice.

One of the most pressing obstacles is the displacement of affected communities, which has become endemic in the areas most profoundly impacted by the conflict. Many individuals who were once able to access legal services are now uprooted, living in makeshift shelters or in areas where their rights are even more vulnerable. This displacement not only fractures the connection between victims and the legal support they need but also complicates the already intricate logistics for CSOs striving to reach them. The loss of physical proximity means that vital information can be lost, leading to delayed responses when legal aid is most needed. Legal practitioners find themselves needing to adapt rapidly to shifting demographics, as the flow of internally displaced persons alters community compositions almost daily. In these moments of transformation, civil society organizations often step into the breach, providing not just legal assistance but also humanitarian aid. They assume the role of lifelines, bridging the gap between victims and the elusive promise of justice, yet this dual focus diverts scarce resources, leaving them stretched thin at a time when proximity and speed of response are paramount.

Moreover, the issue of inadequate funding poses a significant challenge, rendering many well-meaning initiatives under-resourced and thereby ineffective. While international funding and support might be available, accessing these resources often requires navigating bureaucratic red tape and adherence to the stipulations that accompany foreign aid. Many CSOs are forced to fight an uphill battle for financial sustainability amid a backdrop of urgent need. Their reliance on grants and donations, which can fluctuate depending on donor fatigue from conflicts elsewhere or shifts in philanthropic priorities, positions them precariously, pushing organizations into a perpetual state of uncertainty. This is compounded by the fact that local fundraising mechanisms have withered under the pressures of conflict, as insecurity deters potential donors and erodes public trust. The cycle of dependency on external funding thus creates an environment of instability, where organizations could potentially have their capacity to provide critical legal support undermined by the very crises they wish to address. Consequently, vital programs may be shelved or scaled back in response to financial strains, leaving beneficiaries in limbo, lacking the legal recourse essential to confronting their challenges.

Additionally, the political climate in Cameroon poses a significant barrier to civil society organizations working within the Anglophone regions. The government has often demonstrated a suspicious disposition towards CSOs, viewing them as potential threats rather than partners in development. This antagonistic relationship manifests in various ways, including excessive regulation and monitoring aimed at stifling free operation. CSOs may face bureaucratic hurdles that include unfavorable licensing conditions, leading to operational difficulties that can further delay responses to legal needs. The climate of suspicion creates a chilling effect, where organizations may self-censor or withdraw from advocating for essential reforms or protections for fear of reprisals or government scrutiny. Legal practitioners within these organizations often operate with the knowledge that exposure could lead to targeted violence or intimidation, compelling them to seek ways to mitigate risk that may inadvertently compromise the effectiveness of their advocacy work. Consequently, the legal needs of affected populations can become overshadowed by the need for CSOs to safeguard their members, resulting in fewer legal resolutions and a perpetuation of the status quo of injustice.

Equally troubling is the dearth of trained legal practitioners willing or able to engage in this dangerous environment. As the conflict exacerbates, many lawyers face the dilemma of continued involvement in a system fraught with risk or opting for self-preservation. The prospect of representing clients in cases riddled with political implications becomes a perilous venture, leading to a significant reduction in available legal aid resources. Those courageous enough to remain active often find themselves in situations where their legal training is tested against laws that shift constantly amid the tumult of conflict, rendering their expertise almost obsolete in certain contexts. The spiraling fear of violence against legal practitioners dissuades many from engaging, particularly those whose families may become targets due to their professional choices. The ripple effects of this exodus reverberate through civil society organizations; with fewer legal practitioners active on the ground, advocates are faced not only with greater workloads but also a knowledge gap that can further enfeeble their ability to serve their clients effectively. As a result, the backlog of unmet legal needs swells, and many victims of the conflict remain unable to access even the most basic services.

In response to these obstacles, civil society organizations have showcased remarkable resilience and innovation. Faced with overwhelming circumstances, many have adapted their operational strategies to better meet the needs that continue to evolve. For instance, some CSOs have taken a proactive approach to community engagement, ensuring that local populations are educated on their rights and the available routes for seeking justice, even in dire situations. Through workshops, community forums, and outreach programs, these organizations seek to empower individuals, cultivating a sense of agency among victims who may otherwise feel entirely disenfranchised. By equipping community members with knowledge, they foster a culture of resilience that can withstand the pressures of the ongoing conflict. This kind of engagement not only helps to maintain hope but is crucial for addressing the justice vacuum that has spread like a blight across the Anglophone regions.

Ultimately, the challenges facing civil society organizations in the Anglophone regions of Cameroon reflect a broader narrative that speaks to the intersection of law, conflict, and human rights. The relentless pursuit of justice, despite the overwhelming odds, emphasizes the indomitable spirit of those who refuse to relent in their fight against injustice. As these organizations navigate the treacherous landscape marked by displacement, funding shortages, political hostility, and a lack of resources, they also exemplify the resilience of the human spirit. Their efforts illuminate the critical need for solidarity among legal practitioners, local advocacy networks, and international partners to forge pathways for reform against the backdrop of crisis. In doing so, they not only strive to restore a semblance of justice but also lay the foundation for a more robust legal system that can withstand future challenges and safeguard the principles of equity, fairness, and humanity for all.

Chapter 7:

Voices of Victims

7.1 Testimonies of Injustice

In the heart of the Anglophone regions of Cameroon, the haunting whispers of injustice echo through the lives of countless individuals who have found themselves ensnared in a legal abyss. Their stories, rich in emotion and laden with sorrow, offer a poignant glimpse into the heart-wrenching realities faced by victims in the midst of a relentless crisis. Each tale is a testament to the human spirit's capacity for resilience in the face of overwhelming adversity, yet it also serves as a stark reminder of the profound failures of a judiciary increasingly rendered impotent by the brutal conflict that engulfs their society.

One such story unfolds in a small village, home to a man named Samuel, whose life was irrevocably shattered during a government crackdown on suspected separatist activities. A father of three and a community leader, Samuel was well-respected and known for his advocacy for peace and understanding among conflicting groups. However, his commitment to dialogue placed him squarely in the crossfire of a military operation that left many innocent civilians apprehended or worse. On that fateful day, as he stepped outside to inquire about the commotion, Samuel found himself surrounded by armed soldiers. Accused of collaborating with the separatists without any substantial evidence, he was swiftly apprehended. His cries for justice fell on deaf ears as he was dragged from one military detention center to another, his rights trampled under the weight of arbitrary accusations. For weeks, Samuel languished in an overcrowded cell, suffering not just the physical abuse from guards but the emotional torment of uncertainty regarding his fate. It was only after a prolonged prison sentence, during which he was denied any legal representation, that he was released due to the growing international pressure on the government—a release marked by the scars of trauma that would forever haunt him and his family.

The tragedy of Samuel's story is not an isolated one; it resonates powerfully with that of Esther; a young woman whose plight encapsulates the gendered dimensions of the legal failures during the ongoing conflict. As a college student in Bamenda, Esther had dreams of becoming a lawyer and advocating for the rights of her community. Yet, her aspirations were abruptly cut short when she was caught in the chaos of a protest against police brutality. During the clash, a group of armed men took advantage of the chaos, and Esther was violently assaulted and subsequently left incapacitated on the streets. The aftermath was a horror of disclosure and betrayal—when she bravely sought justice, raising her voice against her attackers, she was met with cold indifference. The police, instead of rallying to her defense, accused her of inciting violence. Her attempts to file a report were thwarted at every turn; the very system designed to protect her instead victimized her further. Esther's testimony is reminiscent of the deep-rooted challenges many women face, battling societal stigmas in addition to a failing legal system that deprives them of a place to seek justice. For Esther, the journey through a corrupted legal landscape is a painful reminder that systemic failures often exacerbate the violence that women endure during times of crisis, diminishing their quest for justice to mere whispers lost in the winds of a turbulent political landscape.

The stories do not end with Samuel and Esther but weave through towns and villages, wrapping around the lives of ordinary citizens who have found themselves threatened by unbridled impunity. Take, for instance, the account of one Njei, a farmer who had dedicated his life to cultivating crops for his community. When soldiers requisitioned his farm for military operations, seizing his land without compensation or due process, Njei faced an uphill battle to reclaim what was rightfully his. His relentless pursuit within the court system was met with hostility. Judges who would normally preside over such matters were either too fearful to act, encountering threats to their safety, or were entirely absent, having fled the region in search of a safer existence. In the absence of fair judgment, local power dynamics shifted, favoring those with links to the armed forces or corrupt officials. Each day, Njei returned to the ruins of his farm, the fertile land now scarred by conflict, quietly mourning the loss of his livelihood while grappling with the harsh realities of a disrupted legal order that left victims like him powerless. Engaging community elders to advocate for his cause proved futile; they were unable to mitigate the growing violence or be heard, their authority diminished by the very forces they once relied on. Ultimately, Njei represents not only the economic devastation inflicted by the conflict but also the profound disruption to community ties and the silent cries of those who are robbed of their rights and dignity.

For many legal practitioners like Sarah, a dedicated attorney who remains steadfast in her commitment to justice, the crisis presents a moral and professional quagmire. As conflict rages around her, she finds herself navigating an increasingly hostile environment while working alongside fellow lawyers who have been threatened or displaced. Sarah's own office was set ablaze during a demonstration, erasing vital documents as well as the hopes of countless clients who sought her counsel. She recalls countless nights spent in overcrowded makeshift legal clinics, where she listens to the heart-wrenching testimonies of individuals—many of whom are traumatized, desperate, and disillusioned. In attempting to defend her clients, she faces the daily dilemma of whether to risk her safety amid threats from both state forces and armed groups alike. The collapse of the rule of law not only places Sarah's professional life at stake but also thoroughly deconstructs the very foundation of trust necessary for a functional legal system. Her journey illustrates the immense pressure facing legal practitioners attempting to grapple with the fallout of conflict, while navigating a fractured societal landscape that has lost sight of justice.

The tales of injustice intertwine to form a vivid tapestry depicting the suffering and resilience of a population determined to seek recognition despite the overwhelming odds. Each individual's testimony contributes to a collective narrative that illuminates the multifaceted consequences of the crisis on the legal system and the deeply ingrained experiences of those who bear the brunt of injustice. As these voices rise, echoing in anguish, their stories imprint an urgency that demands action and reform, urging stakeholders to listen, to understand, and to advocate for the restoration of justice in the Anglophone regions of Cameroon. The recognition of their experiences serves as a crucial reminder that the journey through a broken legal system is not just a bureaucratic problem; it is a human rights crisis that necessitates immediate attention, engendering a call to restore hope in the hearts of the displaced, the traumatized, and the silenced.

Justice, in essence, must be more than a word; it must become the bedrock upon which families like Samuel's and communities like Esther's can rebuild lives torn apart by the ravages of conflict. The testimonies captured here are more than mere accounts; they are a plea to honor the fundamental right to justice for all, an entreaty to rekindle the flickering flame of hope, and a call to ensure that in the crossfire of ongoing strife, the voices of the most affected do not fade into complete silence—so that a future grounded in equality and fairness can be crafted anew.

7.2 Seeking Redress

In the heart of the Anglophone crisis, deeply embedded within the humanitarian turmoil, lie the stories of those who have faced extraordinary challenges in their pursuit of justice. Seeking redress in a fractured legal system is not merely a matter of filling out forms or pleading before a judge; for many victims, it is a perilous journey fraught with despair, fear, and countless obstacles. The testimonies of individuals who have suffered injustices unveil the dire consequences of the disintegration of the judicial framework, illuminating the often-unseen human cost of a crisis that has rendered ineffectual the very institutions designed to protect their rights. Consider the narrative of Kemi, a young mother caught in the crossfire of violence when armed groups clashed with government forces, leaving her home in ruins and her livelihood shattered. After witnessing the loss of her husband during one of these violent skirmishes, Kemi sought legal help to obtain justice for his death, believing against all odds that the system could support her. Her journey, however, quickly revealed the obstacles she would face at every turn. The courthouse she once frequented had become a ghost of its former self, its imposing walls now marred by bullet holes and silence. With no access to legal representation, Kemi was left to navigate the labyrinth of legal jargon alone, often forced to confront officials who were indifferent to her plight. Each visit to the ruins of the courtroom was a painful reminder of her loss, compounded by the realization that her cries for justice were met with deaf ears.

In another part of the region, we hear the story of Emil, who had the misfortune of being in the wrong place at the wrong time. He was arrested following mass detentions, targeted not for any crime he committed but rather simply for being a part of a community suspected of harboring dissent. Emil's attempts to seek redress were met with obstacles that seemed insurmountable. After enduring days of detention without charges, his efforts to pursue legal action against the police were met with harassment and intimidation. Each attempt to file a complaint was met with a bureaucratic black hole that seemed engineered to deny him justice. His family lived in constant fear, knowing that Emil's quest for accountability could not only jeopardize his safety but also expose them to retribution. Tragically, his experience is not unique; in a system teetering on the brink of collapse, countless citizens like Emil find their voices suppressed, their rights forfeited in the name of maintaining a fragile order. The despair grows more palpable as we shift to recounting the testimony of Amina, a local lawyer who, despite her dedication to the rule of law, has been rendered nearly powerless due to the chaos. As courts ceased to function normally and countless judicial officers were displaced, Amina found herself at a crossroads, having to balance her commitment to her clients against the very real risks to her life. The tension between her professional responsibilities and personal safety became a daily struggle. She painted a vivid picture of the limitations imposed upon her, as she faced not only the disruption of the judicial system but also violent threats from both state and non-state actors.

Seeking redress in this context becomes not merely a legal issue but a survival battle, where victims are often left vulnerable and unprotected. The life stories shared in this chapter reveal a chilling pattern of impunity and despair, where recourse is elusive and justice is but a distant dream. The psychological toll of this struggle is profound—victims of the Anglophone crisis carry with them not just the emotional scars of their experiences but also the weight of a justice system that has become an instrument of fear rather than a means of protection. What emerges from these narratives is a complex tapestry of hope and hopelessness, where the aspiration for justice coexists with the harsh reality of a broken system. The voices of individuals speak to something much larger than their individual stories; they reflect a collective anguish and a yearning for a judiciary that can reclaim its role in society. Against this dire backdrop, the themes of resilience and determination are woven in and out of their struggles. Some citizens, despite being battered by the harsh winds of injustice, continue to seek assistance from civil society organizations, desperately hoping they can provide a pathway to appellate justice, a thread of legal optimism dangling in the darkness. The role of CSOs, as they strive to provide legal support, has become paramount in these moments of crisis, yet they too operate within a landscape of constraints marked by limited resources and constant threats.

The narratives we encounter are not solely tales of despair but they also evoke moments of solidarity and community. Such accounts remind us that even amid profound injustices, there are glimmers of hope—instances where individuals have organized grassroots movements, calling for accountability and reform. In these moments, Kemi found kinship among other victims, their collective cries for justice echoing in the spaces that had once been deserted. They established networks to share their experiences, which not only helped in drawing attention to their plight but empowered them to seek legal redress as a united front. The journey of seeking justice is inherently fraught with challenges, but it is also a reminder of the strength found within the community. Amina, rather than succumbing to hopelessness, began to engage in community outreach, assisting those who had intersected with the justice system yet had been overlooked. She advocated not just for the individuals she represented but for a systemic change that could restore faith in the judiciary.

In the backdrop of these poignant stories is the undeniable truth that the quest for justice is ultimately about empowerment, recognition, and restoring the sanctity of human rights. Each story captured here is emblematic of a broader narrative that speaks to the necessity of a functioning judiciary in preserving societal order. They amount to a powerful testimony that, even in the darkest of times, the human spirit's yearning for justice remains unquenched. The obstacles faced by Kemi, Emil, and Amina are a clarion call for stakeholders and policymakers alike, emphasizing the urgent need to restore the rule of law in Cameroon. For while the scars of the Anglophone crisis may run deep, the stories of those seeking redress remind us of the fundamental right that resides in every individual—the right to seek justice and the right for it to be served. As we reflect on their journeys, we are compelled to ask profound questions about our responsibilities to ensure that no one is left behind in the quest for justice, especially in times of crisis. The pursuit of redress in the Anglophone regions serves as both a tragic indictment of the current state of affairs and a hopeful reminder that every effort to reclaim a semblance of justice is a step toward rebuilding the foundations of society fortified by the rule of law.

7.3 Resilience and Hope

In the midst of the turmoil enveloping Cameroon's Anglophone regions, the human spirit's resilience shines through the bleakness, illuminating the narratives of individuals whose lives have been profoundly interrupted by the current crisis. These individuals, marked by the scars of injustice, rise from the ashes of despair, their stories echoing the bittersweet complexities of survival in a fractured legal landscape. Each testimony is a testament to the struggles not just for justice, but for dignity, hope, and the possibility of restoring a semblance of normalcy in the midst of the chaos surrounding them. To understand the depth of this resilience, one must peer into the lives of those who have encountered relentless barriers in their quest for justice, grappling with the harsh realities imposed by both conflict and a crumbling legal system.

Take, for instance, the story of a woman named Amina, a teacher and mother of three who once flourished in her community as an educator. Her life took a tragic turn when violence erupted around her, leading to the unlawful detention of her husband during a government crackdown on perceived dissenters. Fearing for her family's safety and struggling to piece together the fragments of her semblance of a life, Amina navigated a labyrinth of military roadblocks, bureaucratic indifference, and rampant corruption as she sought legal assistance. Amina's journey through the intricacies of an overwhelmed judicial system is rife with obstacles: she confronted judges who were either too terrified to partake in trials or were operating from makeshift courts with no semblance of legality. Despite the nightly tremors of fear that gripped her heart, Amina steadfastly held onto her hope, even as she witnessed the slow erosion of her rights. With every obstacle, she found her resolve hardening; her plight transformed into a cause for others, connecting her with fellow victims who shared similar grievances, thus fostering a nascent community of resilience where there was once only despair. Through the bonds of shared suffering and mutual support, Amina discovered purpose, lending her voice to the unspoken tragedies of others while forging pathways toward justice at great personal risk. Similarly, the journey of Samuel, a young lawyer caught between the demands of his profession and the perils of a society in disarray, serves as another poignant illustration of resilience. Following the outbreak of hostilities, Samuel faced a grim reality where legal practitioners like him became targets in their own right; judges were displaced, legal resources dwindled, and clients became increasingly reluctant to seek justice for fear of reprisal. Each case Samuel took on became an intimate exploration of human suffering, revealing the generational effects of a system on the brink of collapse. Despite the constant threats, the intimidation tactics, and witnessing first-hand the agony of his clients, he chose to fight. His advocacy became more than just a matter of legal obligation; it burgeoned into a lifeline for those struggling for their rights amid the suffocating injustice surrounding them. Samuel organized community outreach initiatives, educating citizens on their rights while gathering testimonies from victims, and pooled resources with local CSOs to provide legal assistance to those unable to navigate an increasingly hostile environment. His resilience became a clarion call, a spark of hope igniting within the community where silence had taken root. Throughout this turmoil, Samuel nurtured the belief that legal representation could be a beacon of hope and solidarity, imbuing those with seemingly insurmountable challenges with the strength to confront their oppressors.

Even as the legal system struggles against a backdrop of chaos, the narrative of Emmanuel, a former Judge who fled to safety after threats to his life escalated, reveals a different dimension of resilience. Forced to abandon the bench due to his refusal to issue unjust verdicts, Emmanuel's story underscores the perilous choices judicial officers had to make in a rapidly deteriorating state where principles were pitted against survival. In exile, his journey did not end; instead, he became a passionate advocate for those left in limbo by the shattering of the legal order. His reflections on the judicial oath he once took reverberated in his advocacy work as he navigated new avenues to uphold the ideals of justice, even outside the confines of a courtroom. Emmanuel engaged with human rights organizations, leveraging his insights to raise global awareness about the plight of Cameroonian citizens—a courageous act that came with its packs of risks and fears. Each meeting he attended, each forum he spoke at breathed life into the notion that he and others were not mere victims of injustice, but skilled advocates aimed at reclaiming the foundation of the rule of law. His story galvanizes a hope that a functioning judiciary can and must survive, pressing for international support to foster change and restoring dignity to degraded lives.

Through these powerful testimonies, it becomes clear that the resilience displayed in the face of adversity is intrinsically tied to the deep human desire for connection, understanding, and justice. The community resilience emerging from unexpected places reflects the strength of shared experiences. In the midst of severe challenges, individuals find solace in their collective identities as victims and advocates—crafting a new narrative that escapes the confines of despair, redefining what it means to seek justice in a world where it has been obscured. It is this very hope that buffers them against despair and propels them forward; the idea that even in the darkest times, the possibility of justice remains a legitimate hope, a fuel for relentless perseverance. Each story is interwoven within a larger tapestry of survival, revealing the struggle for dignity in moments of vulnerability, emphasizing that resilience in the face of chaos is as much a human right as the right to justice itself. It is within this arduous journey through the legal system that hope emerges victorious, binding the community in solidarity and igniting a movement for change that extends far beyond the borders of the Anglophone crisis, confronting injustices that resonate globally. In confronting their stark realities, individuals such as Amina, Samuel, and Emmanuel epitomize a resounding spirit that pushes against the tides of injustice, illuminating the path toward reform through personal sacrifice and collective action. Their experiences serve as haunting reminders of the human cost of conflict. They unveil the ongoing struggle for justice to foster a world where empathy and action merge to restore dignity, sanity, and the rule of law. It is this unwavering resilience that not only withstands the trials of adversity but also lays the groundwork for the future, creating a conduit of hope for the next generation yearning for change. With every voice echoing the resounding plea for justice, it becomes increasingly evident that the human capacity to endure and overcome is inseparable from the fight to restore a fractured legal system. As the narrative unfolds, it is apparent that through resilience, hope thrives, kindling a relentless spirit aimed at reshaping the contours of justice in Cameroon while providing an enduring blueprint for understanding the implications of adversity in the struggle for rights, dignity, and humanity.

Chapter 8:

Judiciary under Siege

8.1 Institutional Weaknesses

The Cameroon judiciary has sustained profound vulnerabilities that have exacerbated the already precarious state of the rule of law in the Anglophone regions. These weaknesses stem from a confluence of historical neglect, political interference, and systemic inefficiencies that have become starkly evident with the current crisis. One glaring issue is the political manipulation of judicial institutions. Over the years, the judiciary has not been insulated from the maelstrom of political influences. This absence of independence has led to a compromised judicial integrity; judges and magistrates often find themselves on a precipice where their decisions can result in dire consequences for their careers, especially when they veer towards anything interpreted as dissent against the prevailing political regime. The specter of intimidation looms large, causing judicial officers to prioritize political expediency over their ethical and professional obligations. When the very arbiters of justice are subjected to such pressures, the implications for the rule of law are chilling. Citizens lose faith in the capacity of the judiciary to render fair and impartial judgments, and thus, the overarching principle that justice must be served without fear or favor becomes an illusion rather than a reality.

Moreover, corruption has all but seeped into the fabric of the judiciary in Cameroon. With inadequate salaries and resources, many judicial officers have been left vulnerable to the temptations of corruption. The rampant bribery wherein litigants must often 'grease the wheels' to secure even the most basic judicial services, not only represents a direct affront to justice but also engenders deep societal cynicism toward the legal process. Litigants, often low-income individuals or those marginalized by the system, find themselves ensnared in a web of transactional justice that prioritizes financial capital over truth and fairness. This commodification of justice undermines the principle that legal redress should be accessible to all – a fundamental tenet of human rights. When those seeking justice must negotiate the perilous landscape of bribery, it deepens societal divides and fosters mistrust among community members who may perceive the legal system as a tool wielded by the privileged few rather than a mechanism of equitable justice.

Another significant contributing factor to the systemic weaknesses within the judiciary is the inadequate training and professional development of legal practitioners. Legal education in Cameroon has been marked by a lack of rigorous academic scrutiny and a shortage of resources for emerging legal minds. As a result, many judicial officers and lawyers who ascend to their positions lack the necessary skills and competencies to effectively navigate the complex legal landscape of contemporary Cameroon. In conflict scenarios like the ongoing Anglophone crisis, the failure of jurists to properly understand and apply international human rights standards has led to numerous violations and miscarriages of justice. The imprisonment of individuals without trial or adequate representation, widely reported under the guise of national security or public order, becomes commonplace, as officers of the law lack the cognitive framework to challenge such injustices within their own ranks. The consequences are dire, as the principle of due process becomes severely compromised, stripping individuals of their basic rights and pushing them further into the shadows of legal recourse.

The judicial infrastructure itself is in disrepair, an outcome of years of neglect and violence. Many court buildings in the Anglophone regions have been damaged or completely destroyed due to the ongoing conflict, rendering many judicial services inaccessible. Displaced judicial personnel often struggle to find appropriate venues to hold court proceedings, leading to significant delays and backlogs in the justice system. This administrative chaos creates a perfect storm that exacerbates the existing weaknesses in the judiciary. Citizens, already distrustful of the judicial process, may choose to abandon their legal claims altogether when faced with such insurmountable obstacles to justice. As courts become ghost buildings, where the sound of a gavel is replaced by the echoes of conflict, the symbolic representation of justice stands eroded, isolating the people even further from the legal system.

Moreover, social and cultural dynamics in the Anglophone regions entail additional layers of complexity that contribute to the judiciary's susceptibility to failure. Traditionally, many communities in Cameroon have relied on customary law and local conflict resolution mechanisms to address disputes. These practices, while having historical significance, have often come into conflict with formal judicial processes, particularly regarding issues of gender, inheritance, and land rights. The increasing resort to local mechanisms in the absence of functioning legal recourse has led to further fragmentation of the justice landscape. Disparities between customary law and civil law create confusion among citizens regarding which legal framework governs their disputes. Women and marginalized ethnic groups frequently find themselves at a disadvantage when navigating both systems, which often favor traditional power dynamics and patriarchal norms. In times of conflict, where the formal legal system is compromised, these disparities are magnified, often resulting in cyclical cycles of injustice that perpetuate social inequities.

The illustrative narratives of judicial officers, lawyers, and ordinary citizens caught in this turbulent crossfire paint a somber picture of desperation and dystopia. Each story encapsulates the broader narrative of institutional weakness, revealing the toll exacted on individuals striving to reclaim their rights within the ruins of a crumbling legal framework. A displaced Judge recounts the harrowing experience of being forced from the courtroom, lamenting how the disruption of his professional life has left him feeling bereft of purpose. His reflections reveal not just personal loss but the larger existential crisis facing the Anglophone judiciary, where the absence of institutional support translates into a palpable sense of hopelessness. A young lawyer passionately shares the struggles of representing clients whose voices have been muted by a system too afraid to confront its own failures. These first-hand accounts underscore the urgency of addressing the judiciary's weaknesses, as they reveal the very human cost of living in a state where justice is elusive.

The understanding of the legal profession as a social contract between the state and its citizens is further strained under the scrutiny of the Anglophone crisis. The role of the lawyer is not merely that of a defender but a protector of rights, positioned to champion justice on behalf of clients who would otherwise be voiceless. Yet, with the judiciary's institutional weaknesses playing out in real-time, it becomes increasingly challenging for legal practitioners to advocate effectively for justice. They operate within a framework that often undermines their role, resulting in a collective disillusionment that marks the entire legal profession. The despair manifesting in their daily experiences reveals how judicial weaknesses can sap the vitality and resolve of dedicated legal practitioners committed to serving their communities.

As the Anglophone crisis marches on, the implications of these institutional weaknesses within the judiciary are far-reaching. A disintegrated legal framework sows seeds of discord, with community members increasingly resorting to vigilante justice or self-help measures as a reaction to the failures of the formal judicial system. The cycle only perpetuates itself, as alternative forms of justice often exacerbate existing tensions, leading to further conflicts and legal disputes. In a society where the capacity to seek recourse through legal means has been eviscerated, the very foundation of civil society is threatened. The voices advocating for justice on the ground become drowned out in the chaos; they know that restoring faith in the rule of law is not merely a matter of legal reform but requires a reassessment of societal values and a re-establishment of trust between citizens and their judicial institutions.

In closing, the institutional weaknesses that plague the judiciary in the Anglophone regions of Cameroon are more than mere administrative or operational inefficiencies but they are indicative of a larger malaise affecting the socio-political fabric of the nation. The intertwining narratives of corruption, political manipulation, inadequate training, dilapidated infrastructure, and cultural misunderstandings create a complex tapestry that reveals how these vulnerabilities contribute to the erosion of the rule of law. Addressing these issues requires a concerted collective effort at both national and local levels, one that prioritizes rebuilding the very institutions designed to uphold justice. As citizens grapple with profound injustices and the loss of legal recourse, the imperative for reform becomes clear, underscoring the critical need for advocates who will not only confront these institutional weaknesses but also champion a vision for a just and equitable legal system responsive to the needs of all Cameroonians.

8.2 Erosion of Trust

In the shadows of the Anglophone crisis in Cameroon, perhaps none have suffered as profoundly as the judiciary itself, eroding the public's confidence in the very institutions that are designed to uphold justice and the rule of law. The courtroom, once a sanctuary where truth was sought and justice delivered, has gradually transformed into a symbol of distrust. For many citizens, the process of seeking justice has morphed from a hopeful endeavor into a perilous journey fraught with uncertainty, intimidation, and disillusionment. With the rising tensions between separatist factions and government forces, the judiciary has found itself ensnared in a web of conflict, often rendering it a pawn rather than an arbiter of justice. As judges, lawyers, and litigants are drawn into the chaos, the very essence of justice—fairness, impartiality, and accessibility—comes under severe threat.

At the heart of this erosion of trust is the systemic displacement of judicial officers and widespread destruction of court infrastructure. Many judges have fled their posts, abandoning the very communities that rely on their oversight and guidance. For those who have remained, the specter of violence looms large, making every day functioning increasingly untenable. Courtrooms that were once hubs of legal discourse have been reduced to empty shells, their walls standing as remnants of a system that once promised protection and recourse. Citizens find themselves grappling with a stark reality where the law seems both distant and irrelevant; they are left to navigate a landscape where judicial officers are nowhere to be found, or worse, where those who remain have been compromised by fear or allegiance to conflicting powers. The consequence of this upheaval is a profound fracture in the public's reliance on the judicial system. As the avenues for redress close off, communities begin to resort to informal mechanisms, often leading to further chaos and injustice. The reliance on traditional or extrajudicial means speaks volumes about the lack of faith in legal proceedings, as citizens increasingly view official courts as ineffective or even hostile environments.

Compounding this crisis is the palpable intimidation faced by lawyers and legal practitioners who bravely attempt to navigate the maelstrom of the Anglophone conflict. In a society where expressing dissent against the state can lead to dire consequences, many legal professionals have found themselves curtailing their advocacy roles, fearing that a steadfast pursuit of justice might put them in the cross-hairs of violence. The chilling effect of such repression manifests in a muted legal community that shies away from taking up cases that may invoke the wrath of either separatist groups or state authorities. The loss of courageous legal representation not only jeopardizes individual cases but also undermines the broader project of restoring the rule of law. As fewer lawyers are willing to take on contentious matters, the voices of the marginalized are silenced, leaving countless citizens without representation or recourse.

Moreover, the collapse of trust extends beyond the judicial officers and practitioners. It pulsates throughout communities, negatively impacting the societal perception of justice. Stories of individuals caught in the crossfire of conflicting interests amplify the pervasive sense of betrayal. Litigants recount harrowing experiences, sharing narratives of how their pleas for justice went unanswered or resulted in further victimization. For instance, one individual described approaching the court to report a violation of their rights, only to find the courtroom completely abandoned, the judge nowhere to be seen. That moment crystallized a profound disillusionment—a realization that the very institution designed to protect them was absent in their moment of need. The resulting frustration from a legal system that seems inaccessible and unresponsive creates an environment where citizens may feel their only option is to resort to self-help, which can lead to cycles of violence and vigilantism.

The implications of this erosion of trust extend beyond the immediate realm of the judiciary and seep into broader societal structures. When a community loses faith in legal frameworks, it begins to question the legitimacy of the government itself. This cycle of distrust can result in increased civil unrest, as frustrations over lack of access to justice turn into actions perceived as rebellion against the state. The risk is not just that individuals lose faith in the courts but that entire communities become disengaged from the democratic processes meant to ensure accountability and justice. The erosion of trust creates a vacuum that invites chaos, with individuals more likely to challenge authority through extralegal means. Additionally, marginalized groups may find themselves further alienated. When access to justice is denied, social bonds fray, and divisions widen.

Navigating the legal landscape has become akin to traversing a minefield, where every step forward is fraught with the possibility of falling prey to the volatility of a failing system. Citizens who once approached the courts with optimism now harbor a subdued sense of resignation. They recount tales of those who sought justice, only to be met with corrupt practices, bureaucratic red tape, or outright hostility. The bartering of justice has become an unfortunate norm, where the highest bidder often prevails. Such a degradation of integrity not only perpetuates injustice but erases the very notion of a fair trial, and the average citizen, once an active participant in their pursuit of rights, begins to view the system as a labyrinthine structure designed to thwart their efforts.

As the Anglophone crisis continues to unfold, the urgency to rebuild trust in the judiciary cannot be overstated. Citizens must see tangible efforts toward reform that address the fundamental issues plaguing the system. This means not just reinstating judicial officers to their posts but also ensuring their safety and infrastructure. It requires a re -calibration of how the legal system engages with communities, restoring faith through transparency, accountability, and genuine redress. Efforts must be directed not only at creating legal mechanisms for recourse but also at building bridges with stakeholders—lawyers, activists, and community leaders—who can forge pathways toward justice in these turbulent times. The question remains: can trust be rebuilt, and if so, how long will it take for communities to feel that their pleas resonate within the judicial systems they once looked to for safeguarding their rights?

The answer may lie in the collective will of a society yearning for justice. It requires understanding that the operation of the legal system is not merely a transactional one but an essential component of a healthy democracy—an institution that exists to serve the people and safeguard their dignity even in times of turmoil. As stories of individual struggles emerge and advocacy gains traction, there lies a glimmer of hope that the tangible rebuilding of trust is possible. The challenges ahead will be monumental, but a concerted effort can pave the way for a judiciary that not only functions effectively but stands as a beacon of hope in the darkest of times. In a country where the scales of justice currently tip precariously, it is imperative that every stakeholder commits to restoring the rule of law and, ultimately, the trust that underpins it. The road may be laden with obstacles, but it is a journey that must begin with the acknowledgment of broken trust and the shared goal of reconstructing a system that upholds justice for all.

8.3 Future of the Judiciary

As the Anglophone crisis continues to evolve, the future of the judiciary in Cameroon rests precariously on a complex intersection of political, social, and institutional challenges. The current state of the legal system reflects not only the immediate consequences of conflict but also the deep-seated issues that have long plagued the judiciary. Emphasizing the need for reform, there lies an opportunity to explore several potential paths for revitalizing the judicial system, restoring public confidence, and ensuring justice is served as a fundamental right, irrespective of the prevailing circumstances. The urgency for reforms cannot be overstated, as the judicial institution stands at a crucial juncture, requiring innovative and practical approaches to navigate the current tumult.

To begin with, one of the foremost pathways to a rejuvenated judiciary involves the reconstruction and rehabilitation of judicial infrastructure. Many court buildings have fallen into disrepair, and some have been entirely destroyed, undermining the ability of citizens to access legal services. Rebuilding these physical structures should be coupled with a commitment to ensuring they are accessible to all, especially marginalized groups who have historically faced barriers in the justice system. This reconstructive effort must extend beyond mere physical renewal; it necessitates the adoption of modern technologies to facilitate the dispensation of justice, such as digital filing systems and virtual court hearings, which could prove invaluable in a context where safety and accessibility become paramount in situations of heightened vulnerability. Furthermore, a robust infrastructure can serve as a symbol of renewed hope for a system that has become synonymous with obstruction and despair.

Moreover, nurturing the human capital within the judicial system is crucial in forging a path toward a future marked by integrity and competence. There is an urgent need for training programs designed to enhance the skills and resilience of legal practitioners working in difficult environments. These programs should focus not only on legal education but also on soft skills such as negotiation, mediation, and trauma-informed practices that recognize the psychological toll of war and conflict on individuals. By fostering a cadre of well-trained legal practitioners, Cameroon can build a judiciary that is not simply reactive but proactive in addressing the needs of its people. Legal professionals, including judges, lawyers, and court staff, must be equipped to navigate the practical and ethical dilemmas present in conflict zones. Ensuring that they understand the role of law in promoting peace and reconciliation could significantly impact their ability to restore order in a fractured system while instilling public trust in the efficacy of judicial proceedings.

A judicial reform agenda must also be firmly rooted in the principles of transparency and accountability. The failures visible in the current system stem in part from a lack of oversight, which has bred mistrust among the populace regarding judicial processes. Establishing independent review boards or commissions that can oversee court operations while providing citizens a channel to lodge complaints about judicial misconduct will enhance the legitimacy of the judiciary. These oversight mechanisms should operate transparently, sharing their findings with the public and implementing feedback systems that inform future judicial practices. By fostering a narrative of accountability, the judiciary can begin to repair the fractured relationship between itself and the communities it serves, allowing citizens to reclaim a sense of agency and empowerment in a system long perceived as adversarial and unresponsive.

Equally relevant is the promotion of alternative dispute resolution mechanisms as a viable option for society contending with the overwhelming pressures of a collapsed judicial framework. In conflict-laden environments, the traditional court system often struggles to keep pace with the ever-increasing backlog of cases. Exploring restorative justice approaches, community-led mediation, and negotiation forums can provide individuals a semblance of justice while alleviating the burden on formal judicial processes. These alternative channels foster engagement among community members and encourage a collaborative journey toward conflict resolution, allowing for a more robust, community-grounded approach to healing and reconciliation. Incorporating local customs and practices can also bridge gaps between the formal court systems and the customary justice practices prevalent in many communities, ultimately enhancing social cohesion and fostering an inclusive atmosphere conducive to rebuilding trust.

As the judiciary contemplates its future, it must not shy away from seeking partnerships with civil society organizations and international bodies dedicated to the promotion of human rights and rule of law. Engaging these stakeholders can amplify the voices of citizens and strengthen advocacy efforts aimed at judicial reform. Civil society plays a pivotal role in monitoring judicial conduct and holding the system accountable while working alongside communities to raise awareness about rights and access to justice. International organizations can lend their expertise and resources to reinforce the efforts of local stakeholders, ensuring that human rights remain central to the discourse surrounding judicial reform. This multifaceted collaborative framework ought to be characterized by belonging, actively involving communities in shaping the solutions that address their unique circumstances, thus fortifying the legitimacy of the reform process.

In the landscape of a disrupted judiciary, addressing the grievance and emotional needs of the populace is paramount. Victims of the conflict have endured significant trauma, and their experiences should serve as the cornerstone of the judicial reform agenda. Initiatives must be designed to validate these experiences, offering platforms for victims to share their stories and access trauma-informed care. By elevating the voices of those most affected by the breakdown of law and order, the judiciary can demonstrate a commitment to healing and restoration, bridging the gap between judicial institutions and the communities they serve. Building a judicial framework where trauma is addressed holistically can facilitate meaningful engagement with the public, empowering them to seek justice and reinforcing their faith in the system.

In light of all these considerations, the future of the judiciary in Cameroon is fraught with challenges yet brims with possibilities for transformation. Embracing these strategic pathways — from rehabilitating infrastructure to fostering accountability, promoting community-based dispute resolution, and engaging in meaningful partnerships — can profoundly reshape the legal landscape and restore faith in the promise of justice. However, such reforms necessitate the collective will of all stakeholders to prioritize justice and the rule of law, recognizing that the judiciary is not merely a system of courts and laws but a vital pillar of society that upholds the dignity and rights of each individual. If embraced, these pathways can lead to a re-imagined judiciary that emerges not as a mere response to conflict but as a driver of peace, equity, and reconciliation, ultimately reinforcing the foundation of a just society where every voice is heard, and justice prevails.

Chapter 9:

International Perspectives

9.1 International Advocacy

In the heart of the Anglophone crisis in Cameroon, the response from international organizations and foreign governments has unfolded in a complex tapestry of advocacy, varying in its depth, commitment, and outcomes. As the conflict escalated, the plight of the Anglophone population caught the attention of human rights groups, foreign ambassadors, and international legal bodies that began to document the pervasive violations of rights and the deterioration of the legal landscape. Organizations such as Human Rights Watch and Amnesty International stepped up their efforts to chronicle the human rights abuses perpetrated in the thick of the chaos. Their reports painted a grim picture of arbitrary detentions, extrajudicial killings, and a systematic dismantling of the rule of law that had left countless citizens vulnerable. These reports were crucial, not only for raising awareness but also for pressuring the Cameroonian government to re-examine its approach to the crisis. The publication of these findings served as a voice for those who had been silenced within their own communities, thus amplifying the international community's responsibility to advocate for their rights.

Support from international bodies came in various forms, ranging from public statements condemning violence to collaborative efforts aimed at restoring peace. The African Union, for instance, expressed concern over the escalating conflict, calling for a thorough investigation into reported abuses on both sides. This call for accountability resonated through diplomatic channels, finding its way into discussions in the United Nations General Assembly and the Human Rights Council. For the first time, discussions about the crisis transcended local borders, with countries that had traditionally overlooked human rights violations in

Cameroon beginning to reconsider their stances on aid and cooperation. Countries such as Canada and the United Kingdom voiced their apprehensions, advocating for a renewed commitment to dialogue focused on finding a sustainable resolution to the conflict. They highlighted the importance of respecting human rights as a precursor to achieving a lasting peace, framing the crisis within a broader narrative of accountability and justice.

The advocacy efforts took on a multifaceted approach, as international legal experts sought to bolster local capacities in delivering justice and ensuring that the rule of law would rebound from its current despair. Workshops and forums were convened, where both local lawyers and international legal professionals shared strategies for holding perpetrators accountable under international law. This collaborative spirit was particularly evident in civil society organizations that drew on international best practices to design intervention strategies tailored to the unique context of the Anglophone crisis. These local entities received crucial support from international donors who recognized that rebuilding the legal infrastructure required both financial resources and technical expertise. The infusion of such resources aimed at creating platforms where victims could share their experiences, thus fostering an environment that prioritizes healing and communal justice. This support did not go unnoticed; the testimonies of those who had suffered often found their way back into international discourse, serving as a constant reminder of the urgent need for change.

Armed with detailed reports and a wealth of testimonies from those affected, advocacy groups began lobbying the international community for sanctions against key figures associated with the violence. Conversations surrounding targeted sanctions against individuals who had perpetuated rights abuses were more than mere diplomatic maneuvering; they were an acknowledgement that access to justice begins with accountability. The dialogue surrounding sanctions, however, was fraught with complications. On one hand, imposing such measures could destabilize already fragile relations; on the other, failing to hold violators accountable could exacerbate the impunity that had taken root in the lifetime of the crisis. The challenge lay in balancing the need for human rights and justice with the geopolitical considerations that colored the relationship between major powers and Cameroon.

In these advocacy efforts, the narrative of justice also birthed a renewed focus on the role of women during the conflict. International advocacy highlighted how women, often on the front-lines of both activism and victim-hood, faced unique challenges in their pursuit of justice and security. Recognizing this was essential for addressing the broader implications of the crisis. The United Nations, through its various agencies, began to emphasize gender-sensitive approaches to conflict resolution and peace-building strategies. This shift recognized that true justice cannot be served without acknowledging the voices of women, who had been marginalized not only by their societal roles but also by the violent turmoil surrounding them. Empowerment initiatives were launched, aiming to provide women with platforms where they could openly discuss their experiences and propose actionable solutions. This holistic approach to advocacy not only enriched the discourse but also inspired a new generation of female leaders committed to championing human rights amid chaos.

Furthermore, international efforts extended to fostering dialogues that included a diversity of voices. Conferences and round-tables were organized, bringing together representatives from civil society, traditional authorities, and diaspora communities. Mobilizing these different stakeholders under one roof created a melting pot of ideas, experiences, and potential solutions for navigating the crisis. These gatherings highlighted a crucial point: while international organizations played a pivotal role in advocating for change, the true path to justice required the active participation of local actors who understood the intricacies of their communities and the ongoing conflict. By emphasizing the importance of localized responses, the discourse shifted towards a more collaborative and sustainable strategy, advocating for a justice system rooted in the cultural nuances of the Anglophone regions.

Despite these advocacy triumphs, challenges remained persistent. Many activists faced backlash for their outspoken positions, particularly when it came to challenging governmental narratives. Intimidation and threats became commonplace for those seeking justice in the shadow of an oppressive regime unwilling to concede to international pressure. Yet, this adversity sparked resilience; local and international advocates banded together, creating coalitions that fortified their resolve. The innovative strategies they employed made use of technology to document abuses and sustain their efforts, even amid escalating dangers. Online campaigns emerged, connecting local voices to global platforms, enabling them to share information, demand accountability, and mobilize support. This digital dimension of advocacy ensured that the stories of those suffering did not fade into obscurity, emphasizing that justice remained an urgent concern, irrespective of the challenges faced.

In conclusion, the international advocacy efforts surrounding the Anglophone crisis in Cameroon evolved to become a powerful tool in the struggle for justice in the middle of an ongoing conflict. These efforts manifested through persistent documentation, calls for accountability, and the mobilization of diverse stakeholders, fostering dialogues that challenged traditional narratives of power. While the challenges are intricate and deeply entrenched, they are not insurmountable. The foundations laid by international advocacy provide a road-map for addressing the complexities of the crisis, urging all stakeholders to align themselves with a vision that prioritizes the restoration of justice and the rule of law in Cameroon. It instills hope, illustrating that global solidarity can amplify local voices, transforming the calls for justice into actions that reshape the future of the Anglophone regions.

9.2 Human Rights Reports

The ongoing conflict in Cameroon's Anglophone regions has drawn considerable attention from international organizations and foreign governments, prompting a flurry of human rights reports that analyze the multifaceted nature of the crisis. These reports vividly outline the extensive violations occurring amid the chaos, detailing systemic abuses that have permeated the legal framework, healthcare access, educational opportunities, and the overall safety of civilians. Organizations such as Amnesty International, Human Rights Watch, and others have painstakingly documented instances of extrajudicial killings, arbitrary detentions, torture, and the disproportionate use of force by security forces. Such organizations have found themselves compelled to not just report on these violations, but also articulate the urgent need for accountability and reform, effectively echoing the voices of those who remain silenced within their own communities.

Central to understanding the collective narrative is the role that these reports play in shaping perceptions at both local and international levels. The intricate weaving of personal testimonies with data-driven insights serves to humanize the statistics that often bombard policy discussions. For instance, a report might not only state the number of displaced persons due to the violence but also recount the harrowing stories of family separation, loss of homes, and the ensuing struggles for survival. Each story underscores the haunting reality faced by those caught between government forces and separatist militants, where access to justice has become a cruel irony. Many victims of violence find themselves navigating a legal labyrinth where the basic rights assured by national and international law are but phantoms, elusive and untouchable in the face of societal collapse.

Moreover, these human rights reports have increasingly emphasized the psychological toll on communities caught in the crossfire. The trauma borne from continuous conflict, compounded by the collapse of legal institutions, leaves individuals grappling with not only immediate fears for their physical safety but also the long-term ramifications on their mental health. Reports detail the acute anxiety and chronic stress faced by those who have lived through violent raids, arbitrary detentions, or the deaths of loved ones. These narratives often incorporate perspectives from psychologists who work on the ground, emphasizing that mental health care remains inaccessible for many. The consequential silence imposed by fear further curtails the community's ability to engage with justice systems or speak out against abuses, thereby reinforcing a cycle of impunity that festers with every unresolved case.

International responses to these human rights reports have varied between strong condemnations and calls for concrete actions. Some governments have pressured Cameroon's leadership to acknowledge the crisis while urging them to halt military action against civilians. However, diplomatic responses often fall short of instigating meaningful change. For every call for accountability, the Cameroonian government has countered with denials and accusations of foreign interference—building a narrative that frames its military operations as necessary to maintain national cohesion. Such rhetoric is often met with skepticism from external observers, particularly when juxtaposed against the stark realities uncovered in investigative reports.

Concurrently, these reports have fostered a sense of urgency among civil society organizations that operate within or outside of Cameroon. CSOs dedicated to human rights advocacy have had to pivot their strategies, moving beyond mere reporting to develop comprehensive frameworks aimed at facilitating real change. This includes documentation intended to support victims' rights through legal channels both locally and internationally. Practical efforts encompass providing legal aid to those who have seen their rights trampled upon and organizing community dialogues to restore trust in what little semblance of the justice system remains. These efforts not only provide immediate relief to those suffering but also plant the seeds for long-term reform, creating a robust platform for dialogue around systemic change in the judiciary.

Documentation alone cannot suffice in the face of mounting evidence; ongoing advocacy is working to position human rights issues at the forefront of political agendas both locally and internationally. The interplay between human rights documentation and the quest for justice exhibits itself vividly in the stories of individuals who have resorted to seeking asylum in foreign nations, carrying with them harrowing accounts that amplify the urgency for widespread reforms. Exile becomes a dual-edged sword; while it offers the safety of distance from conflict, it also dislocates individuals from their roots, stripping communities of their cultural and social fabric.

The international community's engagement with Cameroon's crisis is critical as it can leverage diplomatic pressure to hold actors accountable for their roles in perpetuating violence and violating human rights. Within this framework, the stories told in various reports are not just individual tragedies; they become the collective memory of a community rallying for recognition, justice, and the restoration of hope. These narratives highlight the crucial role that local and international media play in shedding light on the crises, serving as watchdogs and amplifiers of voices that have long been muted.

The call for accountability, as stressed in these human rights reports, serves as a resounding echo that compels us collectively to reconsider what constitutes justice amid upheaval. The types of reform most fervently advocated range from restructuring the judiciary to re-educating law enforcement on human rights best practices. Such measures are interconnected, resonating with a broader understanding that justice is not merely punitive; it must also restore dignity, facilitate reconciliation, and bridge the distance born from fear and mistrust.

This recommendation for reform becomes even more pressing when viewed against the backdrop of a legal institution that is rapidly deteriorating, evidenced by the increased reports of judicial officers being threatened or even executed for their role in upholding the law. Increasingly, judges fear for their safety; their impartiality becomes precarious in a climate of intense scrutiny where decisions are scrutinized through the lenses of loyalty and political affiliation. In this maelstrom, legal practitioners emerge as unwilling participants in a menacing dance of conflict, where the sanctity of law is exchanged for survival, and their very roles become political bargaining chips in a game they never chose to play.

In drawing connections between the content of human rights reports and the lived experiences of individuals on the ground, it becomes apparent that the fight for justice is not just a legal battle; it is fundamentally a human battle. It is about people yearning for recognition, their stories demanding to be told, and their rights clamoring to be safeguarded despite the presence of conflict. As international organizations and foreign governments strive to amplify these voices, it reinforces a collective aspiration—a steadfast commitment to ensuring that even during chaos, the principles of justice remain a guiding star for those navigating the complex legal landscape of Cameroon.

9.3 International Legal Frameworks

The Anglophone crisis in Cameroon has raised essential questions about the applicability of international legal frameworks in addressing conflicts that arise from internal strife and separatist movements. For decades, Cameroon has faced a complex mosaic of issues rooted in colonial history, linguistic disparities, and socio-political disenfranchisement. At the heart of this turmoil, international law stands as a potential beacon for both rectifying injustices and holding accountable those who perpetrate human rights violations. The principles enshrined in various international legal documents, including the Universal Declaration of Human Rights and the International Covenant on Civil and Political Rights, are pivotal in shaping the discourse surrounding the Anglophone crisis. They affirm the significance of protecting individuals' rights regardless of their nationality or the conflicts in which they find themselves embedded. As the conflict escalated, various international organizations, including the United Nations, the African Union, and countless non-governmental organizations, expressed varying levels of concern regarding the growing human rights abuses within the affected regions. These organizations have frequently called for a cessation of hostilities and sought accountability for acts of violence carried out by both state and non-state actors, signaling a need for reintegration of the principles of justice and the rule of law.

The role of international legal frameworks becomes especially pertinent in situations where domestic systems falter, as seen in Cameroon. The breakdown of courts, the displacement of judges and lawyers, and the obliteration of courtroom infrastructures underscore the urgency of looking beyond national borders for solutions. Scholars and practitioners highlight that under the Responsibility to Protect (R2P) doctrine, the international community has an obligation to intervene when a state fails to protect its population from atrocities. This concept may be increasingly relevant as the crisis unfolds, revealing a humanitarian emergency warranting intervention to safeguard fundamental human rights. The international community's response—including voices from civil society—has been critical in urging the Cameroonian government to seek dialogue with separatist leaders and to prioritize the re-establishment of a functioning judiciary. However, reactions from foreign governments have been inconsistent, often falling prey to geopolitical interests, which complicates advocacy for accountability. Through platforms like the United Nations Human Rights Council, there have been calls for investigations into the alleged war crimes and crimes against humanity committed during the turmoil, though these calls often meet resistance when tied to the notion of sovereignty and non-interference in internal affairs.

Responses to the legal ramifications of the crisis also involve investigating the implications of various international treaties to which Cameroon is a party. The African Charter on Human and Peoples' Rights warrants examination concerning the apparent violations stemming from the Anglophone crisis. Article 24, which emphasizes the right to a healthy environment and an adequate standard of living, becomes particularly significant when contemplating the broader socio-economic injustices suffered in these regions. Direct consequences include the targeting of civilians, arbitrary detentions, and systemic human rights abuses that disregard the inherent dignity due to all persons, irrespective of the circumstances. Compounding these violations is the silence of the judiciary, often rendered ineffective through intimidation and violence in areas most affected by fighting. Each story of stripped rights calls for advocacy in the international arena, where human rights organizations closely monitor and report on the situation, compelling greater international engagement.

Organizations such as Amnesty International and Human Rights Watch have taken a proactive stance, drafting reports that document the egregious violations taking place, providing much-needed visibility in the global sphere. Their relentless work amplifies the voices of the oppressed, fostering a semblance of hope that justice, however delayed, can emerge from the chaos. Though it may not guarantee immediate action, documented evidence can provide a basis for future accountability, as it holds states and non-state actors responsible for their violations before the scrutiny of international law. Meanwhile, the United Nations High Commissioner for Refugees has reported increasing refugee numbers, compelling neighboring countries to grapple with the repercussions of the crisis, further complicating regional legal challenges. Each displaced individual carries a story that cries out for justice, reflecting the cascading impact of failing legal systems under conflict, and highlighting the intersection of international obligations to protect these individuals.

Efforts in the international legal domain also highlight the significant role civil society plays in advocating for reform and protection amid conflict. Grassroots movements engage in fostering awareness and mobilizing support, seeking to bridge local needs with international support for implementing essential reforms that could stabilize the legal landscape in Cameroon. Engaging with international legal narratives aids not just in seeking reparations but also in refocusing local leaders' attention on the profound responsibility they have to their citizens, particularly regarding restoring faith in judicial systems. The intertwining of these narratives fosters an environment where local voices resonate harmoniously within the larger international framework, demonstrating that accountability efforts do not merely rely upon external pressure but also on mobilizing local stakeholders back to the negotiating tables.

These dialogues, however, risk being overshadowed by the realities on the ground as often, the urgency to act clashes with the sluggish pace of international diplomatic efforts. Intriguingly, while international frameworks provide procedural standards, the slow-moving wheels of intervention are compounded by territorial disputes and diplomatic hesitations that place a damper on any swift resolutions. A lack of willingness from influential states to directly engage with the Cameroonian government complicates initiatives aimed at reassessing human rights policies and frames the prevailing narrative as one lacking urgency. Nonetheless, the role of international legal frameworks cannot be understated, as they represent the backdrop against which local stakeholders advocate for necessary changes. They provide a compelling pathway for transitioning the discourse from mere conflict resolution to a profound engagement in restorative justice principles, thereby emphasizing that sustainability hinges on addressing the root causes of injustice and inequity at every stratum of society.

As the crisis continues to evolve, the interplay between local narratives and international attention will shape the future of justice in Cameroon. Advocates, legal practitioners, and civil society organizations must remain steadfast in holding space for dialogues that transcend the immediate fallout of violence while emphasizing the urgent need for comprehensive legal reforms. Whether through engaging with international bodies or amplifying local voices amid the conflict, it is vital to ensure that discussions regarding international legal frameworks remain vibrant and proactive. This interconnected approach fosters not only immediate humanitarian assistance but also lays the groundwork for the long-term advocacy necessary for enduring reforms. The imperative to collaborate across borders and champion the sanctity of human rights encapsulates the essence of true justice—which, if realized, would uplift not only the Anglophone regions of Cameroon but also enhance the likelihood of stability and peace across the region, reinforcing that the quest for justice does not merely belong to one country but is a global endeavor that requires the commitment of all stakeholders.

Chapter 10:

Proposals for Reform

10.1 Policy Recommendations

Restoring the rule of law and improving access to justice in the Anglophone regions of Cameroon require an urgent and thorough re-examination of the existing policies governing the judiciary, coupled with the design and implementation of strategic reforms that address the multifaceted challenges faced by the legal system. A comprehensive approach is essential—one that not only addresses the immediate crises but also envisions a stable and resilient judicial framework that could withstand political and societal upheavals in the future. The following policy recommendations are aimed at revitalizing the judiciary, fostering public trust, and ensuring that justice is accessible to all citizens, irrespective of their geographical or sociopolitical status.

First and foremost, it is imperative to establish a robust framework for the protection and security of judicial officers. The ongoing violence and harassment have led to the displacement of many judges and lawyers, undermining the integrity of the judicial process. The government must prioritize the implementation of security measures for legal practitioners, including the establishment of protective protocols and emergency response systems tailored specifically to safeguard those working within the judiciary. Providing judges with safe working environments is not merely a matter of physical security but also a fundamental prerequisite for maintaining the independence of the judiciary, which in turn reinforces public confidence in legal institutions. Furthermore, training programs focusing on risk management and crisis response for judiciary personnel can enhance their ability to cope with threats and apprehend those attempting to undermine the rule of law.

Justice can only prevail when courts are adequately equipped to serve the public. Therefore, there is an urgent need to assess and rehabilitate the physical infrastructure of the judiciary in the Anglophone regions. Many court buildings have been either abandoned or severely damaged due to the conflict, hampering the delivery of justice. A comprehensive audit of the current state of these facilities is necessary, followed by a detailed plan to restore and modernize court infrastructure. This plan should encompass not just rebuilding physical structures but also ensuring that courts are equipped with the necessary technology and resources, which can vastly improve efficiency and support remote access to justice. Digital platforms for court operations should be prioritized, facilitating online hearings and case management systems that allow citizens to engage with the judicial process without facing physical barriers, particularly in a conflict-ridden environment.

The reform of legal aid services must also be a priority in the quest for equitable access to justice. Many individuals, particularly in conflict zones, are unable to afford legal representation, leaving them vulnerable to exploitation and injustice. A well-structured legal aid system should be established, funded by the government or through partnerships with non-governmental organizations. This system must be decentralized to ensure that services reach even the most remote communities. Moreover, legal practitioners should be motivated to undertake pro bono work in these regions, and measures must be instituted to evaluate the effectiveness of legal aid schemes regularly, ensuring they align with the needs and realities of the affected populations. Easing access to legal knowledge and resources through community education programs, where citizens are informed about their legal rights, can also empower them to seek justice.

Furthermore, addressing the backlog of cases in the courts must be a crucial component of any reform agenda. The Anglophone crisis has generated a significant number of unresolved cases, rendering many judicial proceedings ineffectual and leaving victims without redress. Introducing a system of case management that streamlines processes, provides prioritization mechanisms for urgent cases, and facilitates alternative dispute resolution methods would contribute meaningfully to alleviating the backlog. Training judges and court staff in effective case management techniques and adopting technology-driven approaches to scheduling and tracking cases can lead to more timely resolutions. It is essential to ensure that judicial officers are supported with administrative resources that enable them to focus on the fair adjudication of cases without being overwhelmed by inefficiencies.

Moreover, a responsive and participatory framework for policy making should be established, involving diverse stakeholders including civil society, legal practitioners, and community members in discussions about the future of the judiciary. These stakeholders can provide valuable insights into the real-life implications of judicial policy and help design reforms that reflect the needs of the people. This participatory process can stimulate public interest in the judiciary, hence fostering a culture of accountability and transparency. Engaging with communities through awareness campaigns that educate citizens about their roles in safeguarding justice can galvanize societal support for the legal system and encourage collective efforts toward reform.

The restoration of public trust in the judiciary is tantamount to the overall efficacy of any reforms undertaken. Therefore, comprehensive oversight mechanisms must be developed to monitor the conduct of judicial officers and ensure integrity within the judiciary. Establishing an independent body that investigates grievances against judicial misconduct and promotes ethical standards would serve as a cornerstone for rebuilding public confidence. Transparency in judicial appointments, promotions, and disciplinary actions must be enforced, and the criteria used must be made publicly available. Judiciary-awareness campaigns can be invaluable in informing citizens about their rights and the avenues for seeking justice when they experience injustices.

Additionally, it is critical to integrate human rights principles at every level of the judicial process. Training programs emphasizing human rights law must be instituted for all judiciary staff, fostering a deeper understanding of the intricacies involved in protecting citizens' rights. Establishing partnerships with human rights organizations can enhance the judiciary's capability to uphold justice that reflects universal human rights standards. Involving human rights experts in case deliberations or initiating court clinics focused on human rights issues could also bolster the judiciary's role in advocating for vulnerable populations, thus reinforcing the intersection of law with fundamental human dignity.

Finally, the international community's role cannot be overlooked. Global stakeholders can provide financial and technical support to facilitate the reform processes, ensuring the successful implementation of recommendations made. Sharing best practices and experiences from similar conflict situations in different parts of the world can offer valuable perspectives and innovative strategies to tackle the crisis effectively. Establishing partnerships with international legal organizations that focus on post-conflict judiciary recovery could also help solicit expertise and resources that are crucial for rebuilding the legal framework.

In summary, the restoration of the judiciary in the Anglophone regions of Cameroon requires a multifaceted reform strategy involving protection measures for judicial officers, rehabilitation of infrastructure, implementation of effective legal aid, addressing case backlogs, promoting stakeholder participation, ensuring transparency and accountability, integrating human rights principles, and engaging the international community. Such a comprehensive approach addresses not only the immediate challenges posed by conflict but also lays the groundwork for a resilient judiciary capable of promoting justice, safeguarding rights, and fostering societal healing in the aftermath of the crisis. Only through these transformative actions can the rule of law be reinstated, paving a hopeful path toward a brighter future where justice serves as a cornerstone of peace, stability, and democratic governance in Cameroon.

10.2 Community Engagement

In the intricate web of challenges posed by the Anglophone crisis in Cameroon, community engagement emerges as a beacon of hope and a critical foundation for reforming the legal system. The significance of community involvement in addressing the injustices faced by citizens cannot be overstated. Indeed, without the active participation of local populations, any attempts at restoring the rule of law and improving access to justice are likely to falter. Grassroots movements have historically played an essential role in social change, and in the current climate of upheaval, efforts driven by individuals who are directly affected by the conflict can realign priorities and foster a collective understanding of the urgent need for reform. Communities, as the first line of defense for those seeking justice, can leverage their unique perspectives and local knowledge to advocate for changes that not only reflect their needs but also align with broader goals of legal accountability and integrity.

In many Anglophone communities, local leaders and civil society organizations have mobilized to address the vacuum left by a weakened judiciary. They possess a profound understanding of the local context, which can translate into advocacy efforts that resonate with both policymakers and international observers. This grassroots engagement has manifested in various forms, including community-based legal clinics, forums for dialogue, and initiatives aimed at educating citizens about their rights. One particularly poignant development has been the establishment of informal community courts, where disputes are mediated and resolved according to locally accepted norms and practices. While these alternative mechanisms do not substitute for an official judiciary, they reflect a community's resilience and serve as a crucial stopgap for those left bereft of traditional legal recourse.

Furthermore, engaging communities in dialogues about legal reforms fosters a sense of ownership over the judicial process. When citizens are actively involved in discussions that shape the laws that govern their lives, they are more likely to uphold and respect those laws. This sense of ownership is particularly vital in the aftermath of civil unrest, where disillusionment with the state can lead to widespread apathy. By giving community members a platform to voice their concerns and aspirations, it is possible to counteract feelings of disenfranchisement and instead cultivate a collaborative spirit centered on the rule of law. This partnership between citizens and legal practitioners can yield innovative solutions tailored to the unique challenges faced in the Anglophone regions, such as improving legal literacy, resolving conflicts amicably, and fostering trust in the judicial process.

Additionally, as local communities engage in advocacy for legal reforms, they highlight the human rights implications of the ongoing crisis. Grassroots organizations have been pivotal in documenting abuses and gathering testimonies from victims whose journeys through a fractured justice system reflect broader systemic failures. These narratives serve as powerful tools for arguing the case for reform, as they ground abstract discussions of rights in the lived experiences of individuals. They form an emotional appeal that both intrigues and compels stakeholders at various levels to take notice. Advocating for the restoration of legal frameworks becomes not just an academic exercise or a technical necessity, but a personal mission for many. Activists and community leaders understand that their voices can mobilize the public and empower victims, helping to shine a light on injustices that might otherwise remain silenced in the shadows of conflict.

Moreover, leveraging the experiences of diverse community members can enhance the development of reforms that uphold justice, equity, and acceptance. Engaging marginalized populations—women, youth, and individuals with disabilities—can lead to a more holistic understanding of the justice needs within the Anglophone regions. These groups often face unique barriers in accessing legal resources or representation, and their active involvement in the reform process can ensure that their specific needs are addressed. In this regard, the empowerment of previously voiceless groups can create a ripple effect throughout the community, fostering solidarity and collective action. Young people, in particular, have demonstrated remarkable enthusiasm and creativity in advocating for change; their involvement not only injects new energy into the movement but also prepares the next generation to uphold and champion the rule of law amid ongoing challenges.

In the realm of community engagement, the collaboration between local entities and external actors, such as CSOs and international organizations, proves to be essential. Partnerships can amplify local voices, allowing them to reach wider audiences and resonate with global discourses on justice and human rights. This cross-pollination of ideas and strategies can lead to more impactful advocacy efforts and attract resources needed to sustain reform initiatives. CSOs, for example, can funnel technical assistance, training, and funding to community-led initiatives while ensuring that local needs remain at the forefront of reform agendas. In this interplay, the local becomes intertwined with the global, enhancing advocacy efforts that demand accountability from state actors and push for substantial changes to legal structures.

Contextualizing community engagement within the broader landscape of the Anglophone crisis also underscores the critical importance of fostering resilience. Communities that come together in pursuit of justice are less likely to fracture under pressure; they become bastions of support for one another, allowing individuals to navigate the harrowing paths toward reclamation of their rights. The grassroots movement for justice does not exist in a vacuum; it is a response to the existential threats posed by conflict, but it can also pave the way for a brighter, more just future. The Shared values of justice, equality, and respect become the foundation for rebuilding, and as these values proliferate among community members, they can catalyze groundbreaking changes throughout the region.

As this resilient spirit takes root, it cultivates a culture of accountability and transparency. It shifts the paradigm from passive acceptance of judicial failings to active participation in seeking redress. This transformation can disrupt the cycle of injustice that has perpetuated itself amid the crisis, allowing communities to reclaim their rights and demand the attention of authorities. Transformation is not merely about placing demands on those in power; it is about fostering a consciousness that permeates through society, where individuals are imbued with a sense of agency and responsibility for one another. The strength of community engagement lies not only in its capacity to advocate for reforms but also in its ability to sculpt a more just and equitable societal framework that benefits all.

However, the road ahead is fraught with challenges, as community-led initiatives can face resistance from entrenched interests. Many in positions of power may view these efforts as threats, leading to intimidation and violence against activists and community leaders. The path toward justice reform must therefore include significant efforts to protect those who dare to advocate for change. Protecting community voices, safeguarding fundamental freedoms, and creating an enabling environment for civil society is paramount to ensuring that the momentum generated by community engagement translates into true reform. Advocacy for accountability can realize tangible outcomes only when those spearheading such movements are empowered and protected. In this light, it becomes essential for external actors to remain vigilant and supportive, amplifying community-led efforts while continuously advocating for safe spaces for dialogue and activism.

Ultimately, community engagement is not just a means to an end but it is an integral part of a trans-formative process that seeks to change the very fabric of society during tumultuous times. Through collaboration, resilience, and mutual support, communities in the Anglophone regions can take back their narrative, redefining what justice looks like in a post-conflict landscape. Restoring the rule of law is not merely about re-establishing legal structures; it is about nurturing a collective ethos that values justice as a cornerstone of society. This commitment, engendered through community engagement, will serve as a powerful catalyst in charting a new course for the Anglophone regions—a course that prioritizes justice, equity, and respect for human rights. In the end, it is the courage of individuals rising to confront systemic injustices together that will guide Cameroon toward a brighter, more just future, reflecting the will of its people.

10.3 Building Resilience

In the midst of the turmoil that has engulfed the Anglophone regions of Cameroon, the quest for resilience within the legal system appears as both a daunting challenge and an urgent necessity. The historical wounds that have led to the current crisis run deep, and the restoration of the rule of law requires innovative strategies that reflect the unique socio-political landscape of the region. Resilience is not merely about bouncing back from adversity; it is about evolving in ways that prepare the legal system to withstand future shocks while simultaneously addressing the injustices that have been exacerbated by the ongoing conflict. To achieve this resilience, a multifaceted approach is necessary, engaging stakeholders at various levels—from grassroots activists to high-profile policymakers—ensuring that every voice is included in the dialogue for reform.

One significant area for reform is the establishment of legal aid programs tailored specifically to the needs of the affected populations. Many citizens in the Anglophone regions have found themselves unable to navigate the complexities of the legal system due to a lack of resources, education, or access to information. By creating community-based legal aid systems, which can be staffed by both legal professionals and trained community volunteers, we can empower individuals to advocate for their rights. Such initiatives would not only facilitate access to justice but would also educate citizens on their legal rights and the available recourse mechanisms, fostering a culture of advocacy and legal awareness among the populace. Moreover, incorporating technology into these legal aid programs can significantly enhance their reach and efficiency. Mobile applications and online platforms that provide legal resources, advice, and networking opportunities can bridge the gap between frustrated individuals and the justice they deserve, circumventing many physical barriers imposed by the ongoing conflict.

In addition to bolstering legal access, fostering a vibrant and independent civil society is paramount for embedding resilience within the legal framework. Civil society organizations have the potential to serve as watchdogs, advocates, and educators, holding both state actors and non-state actors accountable for violations of rights during and after the conflict. Empowering these organizations to operate freely, without fear of harassment or retaliation, will create an environment where citizens can engage in constructive dialogue and advocate for accountability and reform. Providing capacity-building workshops and funding opportunities for civil society groups will equip them with the skills necessary to effectively engage with the judiciary, legislative bodies, and the broader community. Furthermore, collaborations between legal practitioners, civil society organizations, and academic institutions can yield valuable research that identifies gaps in the current legal framework and offers innovative solutions tailored to the needs of the Anglophone regions.

Bolstering community resilience in the face of systemic failures also requires a re-evaluation of the role of the judiciary itself. As various judges and judicial officers have been displaced or rendered ineffective, creating programs aimed at reintegrating these legal professionals into the community is crucial. Providing them with the necessary resources to resume their duties—such as security measures, training on conflict-sensitive adjudication, and institutional support—could revitalize the faith the public has in the judiciary as a fair arbiter. It is essential that these judicial officers, having experienced the conflict firsthand, are provided opportunities for trauma-informed practices that recognize the psychological stresses that come with their positions during such turbulent times. Additionally, initiating dialogues between judges and the community could facilitate a better understanding of the challenges that litigants face, leading to more compassionate and informed decision-making that considers the socio-political context influencing their cases.

Moreover, cultivating a restorative justice approach within the legal system can radically transform how communities engage with justice. This alternative to punitive measures fosters healing and reconciliation, thereby promoting social cohesion among communities torn apart by violence. Integrating restorative justice principles into legal proceedings not only encourages dialogue between victims, offenders, and the wider community but also acknowledges the impact of the conflict on relationships and communal structures. Training legal practitioners in restorative justice techniques ensures that even in the face of overwhelming adversity, the principles of fairness and compassion can guide judicial outcomes. This approach recognizes that many individuals in the Anglophone regions have faced tremendous loss, and by prioritizing healing over punishment, communities can begin to mend the fractures inflicted by conflict.

Furthermore, building resilience means creating a culture of accountability where judicial officers can act without intimidation. Safeguarding judicial independence requires not only protection from external threats but also instilling confidence within the judiciary itself. Establishing a transparent mechanism for reporting cases of intimidation or corruption can deter actors from undermining judicial integrity. International partnerships and support can also play a crucial role in reinforcing this independence, ensuring that local judges have the backing of global legal standards that champion justice. The global community, by standing in solidarity with those advocating for justice in Cameroon, can amplify local efforts and contribute resources—financial and technical—that are vital for system reform.

An often-overlooked yet powerful avenue to resilience lies within the stories and experiences of those who have personally navigated the fractured legal system amid crisis. By systematically gathering these testimonies and documenting personal experiences, we not only affirm the struggles faced by individuals but also recognize them as part of a collective narrative that demands attention and action. This documentation serves multiple purposes: it sheds light on the systemic failings that need reform, provides evidence for advocacy efforts, and empowers citizens by validating their experiences and reinforcing their agency in seeking justice. Community-driven projects focused on recording these narratives can strengthen civic engagement, creating a moral obligation for change among the local population and stakeholders alike.

Lastly, recognizing that any sustainable reforms must be inclusive is vital. The voices of marginalized groups—women, children, and the elderly—must be prioritized in discussions surrounding legal reform and resilience-building. Gender-specific barriers that inhibit access to justice for women, often heightened during times of conflict, require targeted interventions that address issues such as domestic violence, land rights, and economic injustices. Policies that ensure representation of women in legal reform processes not only strengthen the voices of those directly affected by injustice but also contribute to a more equitable justice system as a whole. Similarly, engaging youth in these discussions prepares the next generation to uphold the rule of law and advocate for justice, ensuring that the narrative transcends the current crises and fosters a culture of respect for human rights.

The path to building resilience within the legal system in the Anglophone regions of Cameroon is complex and multi-layered, necessitating a communal effort that bridges gaps across societal divides. While the challenges are significant, they are not insurmountable. By re-calibrating the focus towards justice-centrist reforms that prioritize access, accountability, healing, and inclusion, we can take meaningful strides toward restoring the rule of law. This journey is not just about addressing the past but looking toward a future where justice is not just an aspiration but a foundational element of society—a society defined by dignity, respect, and a robust commitment to human rights for all its citizens. In this renewed landscape, resilience becomes not only a goal but a lived reality, where the legacies of the past inform a more just and equitable future for the Anglophone regions of Cameroon.

Chapter 11:

Conclusions and Future Directions

11.1 Key Insights

In assessing the intersection of law and conflict throughout the narrative of the Anglophone crisis in Cameroon, several critical insights emerge that weave together the multifaceted challenges faced by the legal system and the personal stories of those striving for justice in chaos. The previous chapters have laid bare the dire consequences of a collapsing judicial framework, where access to justice becomes an unattainable dream for many citizens in the affected regions. The state of the judiciary, which should be a bastion of hope and fairness, has instead devolved into a lamentable shadow of its former self, marred by violence, intimidation, and displacement. This chapter seeks to consolidate the core findings of this journey, underscoring an immediate need for targeted reforms and revival of the rule of law within the Anglophone regions of Cameroon.

The first key insight relates to the profound impact of conflict on judicial operations and the rule of law. The Anglophone crisis has not only obliterated the physical infrastructure necessary for judicial proceedings—court buildings have been destroyed, and judicial officers forced into exile—but it has also eroded the very fabric of legal accountability. When courts are rendered non-functional and legal recourse becomes a distant hope, it catalyzes a vacuum of justice that leaves an entire populace vulnerable to abuse and exploitation. The narratives of dislocated judges and displaced citizens alike illustrate the disruption of order that ensues when the judiciary succumbs to the pressures of conflict. The erosion of the legal framework propels ordinary individuals into a state of lawlessness, urging them to ponder not only the immediate safety and resolution of their grievances but also the long-term implications for societal cohesion and peace.

Furthermore, numerous experiences shared in prior chapters highlight the chilling effect that violence and intimidation exert on legal practitioners, with many lawyers grappling with the moral quandaries of operating in an environment marked by threats to their lives and livelihoods. These dedicated advocates navigate a treacherous landscape, striving to uphold their professional responsibilities while partially retreating from their roles as defenders of human rights. A poignant reality captures the struggle of any attorney who dares to challenge the status quo during such tumult. As many express, the fragility of judicial independence becomes evident as the fear of retribution looms large, illustrating a stark dichotomy between the ethical tenets of their profession and the perilous backdrop against which they operate. This direct confrontation between duty and fear highlights the urgent need to buffer legal practitioners from the political strife that influences their capacity to serve effectively, helping reestablish the judicial system as a refuge for those in need.

Another salient theme is the amplified vulnerability of women and marginalized groups in this context, as the breakdown of law disproportionately affects those already facing systemic disadvantages. The stories recounted throughout this book illuminate how women, the elderly, and individuals from less privileged backgrounds often find themselves further marginalized when the judicial process is undermined. The absence of legal protections engenders a pervasive culture of silence and victimization, perpetuating cycles of violence and denying many their fundamental rights. The experiences of these individuals compel us to acknowledge that the ramifications of judicial failures reverberate throughout communities, stifling not just individual dreams, but also collective progress towards a just society. In amplifying their voices, the need for equitable access to justice emerges as both a moral and pragmatic necessity in rebuilding trust and stability in the aftermath of conflict.

In forming a comprehensive picture of the current state of the judiciary amid this crisis, it becomes clear that the prevailing judicial landscape is characterized by a lack of clarity surrounding legal rights, obligations, and recourse for victims of injustice. The testimonies documented show that many citizens remain paralyzed by the overwhelming complexity of navigating the legal system while confronted by the stark absence of judicial recourse. Furthermore, the principle of due process is increasingly vulnerable, as the disruption of legal protocols gives rise to arbitrariness in the treatment of cases. The suggestion here is not merely to return to a pre-crisis status but to take an introspective look at how justice is defined and delivered. If the judiciary is to regain its stature as a pillar of society, it must evolve to meet the contemporary needs of the populace while engendering a clearer understanding of rights and responsibilities among citizens.

The final insight delves into the potential pathways for restorative measures that must be pursued to revitalize the judiciary in Cameroon's Anglophone regions. Advocating for legal reforms, capacity building, and accountability mechanisms must be at the forefront of any meaningful effort aimed at reinstating the rule of law. Empowering local judicial officers and establishing safe zones for legal practice could facilitate the gradual restoration of judicial independence and integrity as professionals are anchored in their commitment to justice. Additionally, enhancing community-based legal aid initiatives has the potential to bridge the gap between citizens and the justice system, reclaiming pathways for the voiceless to express grievances and seek redress in a manner that honors their dignity and rights. The collaborative engagement of civil society organizations and local stakeholders can be pivotal in pushing for reforms that resonate with the cultural intricacies of the communities most affected by the crisis. Advocacy must also bring international attention to the persistent failures of the legal system, pressing for external support in building judicial capacity and infrastructure, thus enabling a framework of justice conducive to enduring peace.

In summation, the insights derived from this exploration of the Anglophone crisis serve as a clarion call to reevaluate and restore the judicial landscape in Cameroon. It is a shared responsibility of legal practitioners, civil society, policymakers, and communities to engage in dialogue and action that prioritizes the fundamental tenets of justice. Opportunities for reform must not only focus on restoring functionality but must intertwine efforts to address broader social inequalities and barriers that hinder access to justice for all. Only through comprehensive collaboration can the ideals of rule of law and accountability take root, generating a future where justice is not merely an aspiration but a lived reality for every citizen. As we confront the remnants of conflict, it is imperative that we collectively forge pathways toward a judiciary that embodies resilience, fairness, and advocacy—a judiciary that champions the human rights of all Cameroonians.

11.2 Future Research Directions

As we look beyond the current discourse on justice in the context of the Anglophone crisis, it becomes imperative to delineate pathways for future research that could foster a deeper understanding of the intricacies involved in the interplay between conflict and judicial integrity. One of the most pressing areas for exploration is the impact of conflict on legal education and the training of legal practitioners. Research could investigate how the upheaval in the Anglophone regions has affected law schools and legal training programs, both of which are fundamental to producing knowledgeable and skilled legal professionals. Are current programs effective in addressing the unique challenges presented in a conflict environment? What adaptations have universities and institutions made to curriculum or pedagogical approaches to prepare law students for their roles in a fractured system? By examining these questions, we not only uncover the immediate implications of diminished access to education but we could also gauge the ripple effects on the overall quality of legal representation and advocacy in an already strained judicial landscape.

Moreover, the role of alternative dispute resolution methods in conflict-affected regions represents a fertile ground for academic inquiry. Traditionally, courts have served as the primary mechanism for resolving disputes; however, as the Anglophone crisis demonstrates, the judiciary is in turmoil. Future investigations could further examine community-based mechanisms for conflict resolution, such as mediation or reconciliation practices that thrive on local customs and societal norms. What can be learned from informal processes that have emerged in absence of a working judiciary? Are there culturally specific methods that have proven effective, and how can these be integrated or recognized within a formal legal framework to assist individuals still seeking justice? By appreciating the successes and failures of such alternatives, researchers can contribute invaluable knowledge that may inform policies aimed at governance and social cohesion during and after conflict.

Crucially, another area of focus should delve into the psychological dimensions of accessing justice in the midst of violence and societal unrest. For many individuals navigating through a system that has become increasingly inaccessible, the emotional toll it exacts is profound. Research that engages with lived experiences and psychological impacts, such as trauma and anxiety among both litigants and legal practitioners, would enrich the conversation. How does the perception of law and the judiciary shift among citizens when they perceive these institutions as failing them? What are the coping mechanisms employed by attorneys or judges who continue their work in the face of adversity? This line of inquiry would extend the discourse from a mere legalistic perspective to encompass the broader social fabric affected by judicial crises, emphasizing a holistic approach toward legal reform that includes mental health considerations.

The intersection of rights in the midst of the persistent Anglophone crisis presents another opportunity for profound academic exploration. As we understand that the conflict has marginalized not only justice seekers but has disproportionately affected women and other vulnerable groups, it leads to an urgent need for research that addresses gender dynamics, rights of displaced persons, and specifically the unique challenges faced by children born into such environments of conflict. How are these groups accessing legal recourse, if at all? What barriers do they face, and what advocacy efforts, if any, exist to support them? Insights drawn from this aspect can play a pivotal role in reshaping the legal dialogue around exclusivity and justice, eliciting a need for reform that accommodates all citizens rather than maintaining an elitist legal approach that ignores the marginalized.

Aside from that, examining the role public perception plays in shaping the legitimacy and functionality of the judiciary is also critical. The Anglophone crisis has undeniably strained the relationship between the state and its citizens, particularly in regard to trust in judicial systems. A focus on public opinion surveys or ethnographic studies within affected communities could yield essential insights into how citizens perceive justice and judicial authority. Are they disillusioned, or do they still see value in testing the courts even with the odds? Understanding how societal views regarding the legal system evolve in crisis situations can inform strategies of engagement and restoration tactics that legal practitioners and advocates could employ to foster trust and confidence in the institution when conflict subsides.

Finally, a longitudinal study of outcomes after judicial reforms or interventions once peace is restored would also be significant. As we advocate for rebuilding the legal framework, it is crucial to have a well-rounded understanding of what reforms lead to substantive changes in access, promptness, and fairness of justice. Research that tracks the transfer of successful practices from other conflict-affected nations to Cameroon could offer valuable lessons learned, ensuring that any proposed interventions are grounded in evidence and adaptable to the local context. This could extend into comparative studies with other regions that have faced similar crises and subsequently reformed their judicial mechanisms, honing in on what worked effectively, what did not, and why.

In conclusion, future research directions in the realm of justice within the Anglophone crisis are both diverse and essential for understanding the multifaceted challenges and potential solutions pertaining to the judiciary in conflict. By broadening the conversation to address legal education, alternative dispute mechanisms, psychological impacts, inter-sectional rights, public perception, and the longitudinal effectiveness of judicial reforms, researchers can lay the groundwork for empowering communities and influencing policies that promote sustainable justice. This work will not only provide a historical record of the ongoing crisis but serve as a springboard for mobilizing citizens, practitioners, and policymakers towards a more just future, one where access to justice is recognized as a fundamental human right, resilient in the face of adversity. This is the call to arms we need but the challenge lies in our willingness to respond.

11.3 A Call to Action

In the heart of the Anglophone crisis in Cameroon lies a colossal void, a chasm created by the systematic breakdown of the judicial framework that has long been the backbone of order and justice for its citizens. The collapse of the legal system is not just an unfortunate byproduct of the ongoing turmoil; it signifies a fundamental attack on the rights and lives of millions who depend on the rule of law. The heartbreaking narratives woven throughout this book reveal the intricate intersections of conflict and justice, painting a vivid picture of desperation within the chaos. Yet, as we witness the erosion of legal structures, it becomes increasingly imperative for stakeholders—lawyers, judges, policymakers, civil society organizations, and every concerned citizen—to rise to the occasion and demand for reform. This is not merely a call, but an urgent plea to mobilize collective energies, channeling them towards a restoration of justice, a reclaiming of rights that have been systematically undermined.

The path toward reform is fraught with challenges, but it is also paved with opportunities for transformation—opportunities that must not be squandered. As judicial officers have been displaced, and courthouses reduced to rubble, we find ourselves at a crucial juncture where the resilience of communities shines through the darkness of despair. The legal practitioners who remain steadfast in their commitment to serve inside the tumult have incredible stories to share, their insights illuminating the issues at hand. It is vital that we amplify these voices; they are not mere anecdotes but powerful testaments to the necessity of a functioning judiciary. Stakeholders must endeavor to engage meaningfully with these practitioners, to listen to their concerns, and to advocate authentically for their needs in a reformed system. Through grassroots initiatives and dialogue, the path towards reform can gain traction, rooted in the real experiences of those affected by the conflict.

Moreover, engaging with the judicial crisis necessitates a keen understanding of the broader socio-political context that has led to the current state of affairs. Policymakers, armed with nuanced insights and empirical evidence, can fashion a legislative framework capable of addressing the needs of both the judiciary and the civilian populace. The perspectives of those who have navigated this fractured system—the litigants, the victims—must underpin the discourse. Their experiences should inform the reforms proposed and ensure that they resonate with the lived realities of Anglophone citizens. By adopting a restorative justice approach that emphasizes healing, accountability, and community involvement, stakeholders can create a legal framework that fosters trust and restores faith in a system that has been sorely undermined.

For too long, the voices of those suffering through the Anglophone crisis have been muted, drowned out by the cacophony of conflict. It is imperative that civil society organizations take up the mantle of advocacy, championing the cause of justice reform with vigor and tenacity. These organizations are uniquely positioned to bridge the gap between the citizens and the authorities, serving as conduits for change. Their role must extend beyond mere representation; they must engage in active mobilization, conducting outreach programs that educate communities on their rights, the intricacies of the judicial landscape, and the mechanisms available to seek justice. By fostering awareness and participation, these organizations will empower citizens to demand accountability, engage in dialogue with judicial authorities, and collectively advocate for the reforms needed to restore the rule of law.

Simultaneously, the international community offers a crucial lifeline. Global stakeholders have a moral obligation to recognize the plight of those suffering in Cameroon's Anglophone regions and to lend their voices to the advocacy for judicial reform. Diplomatic pressure, support for human rights initiatives, and funding for capacity-building programs within the judiciary can catalyze meaningful change. Furthermore, the engagement of international NGOs and law firms can bolster local efforts, providing technical assistance, legal resources, and expertise aimed at fortifying the justice system. By pooling resources and forming strategic alliances, the international community can amplify the voices of those fighting for justice and encourage a holistic, cross-border approach to addressing the crisis.

In the narratives of despair, there exists an unyielding spirit of resilience among the community members—families united in their struggle for justice, young lawyers fervently advocating for their clients against daunting odds, and judges clinging to the principles of fairness despite evoking the wrath of opposing factions. These stories of perseverance are not simply anecdotal; they represent the undercurrents of hope which can potentiate significant change. We must build upon this spirit, galvanizing community members to unite in a robust coalition advocating for judicial reform. Collaborations should extend beyond legal practitioners to engage educators, community leaders, and even artists who can utilize their platforms to voice the need for justice and the privilege of rule of law. A multi-faceted approach to advocacy can mobilize diverse constituencies, generating momentum that feeds into larger reform efforts.

It is crucial that any call to action is accompanied by a thorough examination of existing frameworks that govern legal settings in Cameroon. Stakeholders must demand a reassessment of laws that serve to empower rather than inhibit access to justice, and initiatives must focus on reclaiming spaces for judicial processes, restoring courts, protecting the rights of legal practitioners, and ensuring robust mechanisms for accountability. Initiatives aimed at investing in legal education, resources for conflict resolution, and community-based justice programs should garner priority, enabling citizens to seek justice not only through traditional courts but also through community mediation systems that uphold equitable standards.

As we reflect on the challenges outlined within this book, it becomes clear that achieving justice during such tumultuous times is both an aspiration and a necessity. We must not shy away from enacting change and advocating for systems that place a premium on fairness and access to justice for everyone. The consequences of inaction during an era marked by unprecedented conflict could culminate in a future bereft of rights and humanity for generations to come. It is vital to recognize that the struggle for justice is interconnected with human dignity and peace. Restoring the judiciary not only serves a legal function but it underpins the very fabric of society itself.

Therefore, let this be a rallying cry, a challenge to all those who are invested in the ideals of justice and the rule of law to rise up, unite, and act. The stories documented here, from the latitudes of personal suffering to the realms of professional sacrifice, testify to the heart-wrenching consequences of neglecting our legal system in times of conflict. Stakeholders—from individuals who dedicate their lives to legal advocacy to the broader community invested in the outcome of these reforms—must seize this moment to ignite collective action that champions restoration and resilience. There is no time to waste as the path to justice begins with us, and it is our duty to traverse it, hand in hand, until the resounding echoes of justice reverberate once more across the Anglophone regions of Cameroon. Together, we have the power to reclaim a judicial system that reflects our shared values, restores faith in justice, and ultimately paves the way to peace and stability.

References

African Commission on Human and Peoples' Rights. *Concluding Observations and Resolutions on the Human Rights Situation in Cameroon.* Banjul: ACHPR, various sessions.

Amnesty International. *Cameroon: A Turn for the Worse? Violence and Human Rights Violations in the Anglophone Regions.* London: Amnesty International, 2017 (and subsequent reports).

Anyangwe, Carlson. *The Secrets of an Aborted Decolonisation: The Case of the Southern Cameroons.* Buea: Langaa Research & Publishing CIG, 2008.

Atanga, Mufor. "The Anglophone Problem in Cameroon." *Journal of Contemporary African Studies* 29, no. 4 (2011): 1–15.

Cheeseman, Nic, Gabrielle Lynch, and Justin Willis. *The Moral Economy of Elections in Africa: Democracy, Voting and Virtue.* Cambridge: Cambridge University Press, 2014.

Dersso, Solomon Ayele. "The Role of Regional Human Rights Mechanisms in Conflict Situations in Africa." *African Human Rights Law Journal* 17 (2017): 1–25.

Fombad, Charles Manga. "Constitutional Reforms and Constitutionalism in Africa: Reflections on Some Current Challenges and Future Prospects." *Buffalo Law Review* 59 (2011): 1007–1108.

Fombad, Charles Manga. "The Crisis of Constitutionalism and Democratic Governance in Africa." *African Journal of International and Comparative Law* 18, no. 2 (2010): 1–20.

Human Rights Watch. *World Report* (Cameroon chapters, 2018–present). New York: Human Rights Watch.

International Commission of Jurists. *Judicial Independence in Times of Crisis: Global Reports on the Rule of Law*. Geneva: ICJ, various years.

International Crisis Group. *Cameroon's Anglophone Crisis at the Crossroads*. Africa Report No. 250. Brussels: International Crisis Group, 2017 (and subsequent updates).

International IDEA. *Constitution-Building Processes in Africa*. Stockholm: International IDEA, 2014.

Jua, Nantang. "Anglophone Cameroon and the Politics of Belonging." *African Studies Review* 46, no. 2 (2003): 65–85.

Konings, Piet, and Francis B. Nyamnjoh. *Negotiating an Anglophone Identity: A Study of the Politics of Recognition and Representation in Cameroon*. Leiden: Brill, 2003.

Mbaku, John Mukum. *Corruption in Africa: Causes, Consequences, and Cleanups*. Lanham, MD: Lexington Books, 2007.

Nyamnjoh, Francis B. *The Politics of Recognition and Representation in Cameroon: Essays in Cultural and Political Sociology*. Bamenda: Langaa Research & Publishing CIG, 2014.

Okafor, Obiora Chinedu. *The African Human Rights System: Activist Forces and International Institutions*. Cambridge: Cambridge University Press, 2007.

Sriram, Chandra Lekha. *Confronting Past Human Rights Violations: Justice vs. Peace in Times of Transition*. London: Frank Cass, 2004.

Takougang, Joseph, and Mathias Krieger. *African State and Society in the 1990s: Cameroon's Political Crossroads*. Boulder, CO: Westview Press, 1998.

Teitel, Ruti G. *Transitional Justice*. Oxford: Oxford University Press, 2000.

United Nations Human Rights Council. *Reports of the Special Rapporteur on the Independence of Judges and Lawyers*. Geneva: United Nations, various years.

United Nations Office of the High Commissioner for Human Rights. *Reports and Statements on the Human Rights Situation in Cameroon*. Geneva: OHCHR, 2018–present.

Young, Crawford. *The African Colonial State in Comparative Perspective*. New Haven: Yale University Press, 1994.